Adam Smith

ADAM SMITH

Plain Texts from Key Thinkers

Edited by Anthony Kelbrook

PARMA BOOKS, LONDON

First edition 1998

ISBN 1-901678-202

Published by Parma Books,
99 Wallis Road, London, E9 5LN

Printed in Great Britain by
Antony Rowe, Chippenham, Wiltshire

CONTENTS

INTRODUCTION

Adam Smith (1723-1790) was born in Kirkcaldy, Fife. He studied at the universities of Glasgow and Oxford and for twelve years was professor of logic and then of moral philosophy at Glasgow. After resigning his chair he travelled on the continent as tutor to the Duke of Buccleuch. On his return he devoted several years to writing *The Wealth of Nations* and was later appointed Scottish Commissioner of Customs. He died in Edinburgh.

His main work *The Wealth of Nations,* from which all the extracts below are taken, is probably the first sustained and thorough analysis of the workings of the market economy and gives Smith as good a claim as any single person to be the founder of economics. It has two recurring themes: that wealth is created through the pursuit of self interest and that each individual is the best judge of his own interest. In recent years the collapse of the Eastern bloc and the resurgence of confidence in capitalism has led to a renewed interest in Smith. The extracts which follow have been chosen for their resonance within related contemporary political debate.

The Division of Labour

That human beings adopt specialised occupations (the "division of labour") and do not attempt to supply all their needs individually is an obvious fact and a familiar observation. No theoretical difficulty is therefore likely to be found in Smith's first chapter. He illustrates the division of labour with reference to the manufacture of pins. He summarises its advantages as "the increase of dexterity in every particular workman; secondly to the saving of time which is commonly lost in passing from one species of work to another; and lastly, to the invention of a great number of machines which facilitate and abridge labour and enable one man to do the work of many." He justifies this last claim by pointing out that the more that a person's work is reduced to a few simple operations the easier it will be for him to imagine ways in which it might be performed by machinery. What is important is to understand why Smith introduces his book with a discussion of the subject. The second chapter points out that the division of labour is intimately connected with exchange. We can concentrate on a single occupation only because whichever of life's necessities that occupation does not directly provide can be bought (or otherwise exchanged) from other people. The *Wealth of Nations* is, at its simplest, a study of the workings of the market economy. Without exchange there can be no market and it is natural for Smith to begin with a subject so central to exchange as the division of labour.

On Protection and the Labour Market

In this chapter Smith attacks regulation, and other interferences in the market, with respect to employment. The particular institutions and practices he attacks are now archaic but still may be thought to have contemporary equivalents. His three targets are apprenticeships, educational subsidies and restrictions on mobility. Smith's attacks on apprenticeship (on the legal requirement that a seven year apprenticeship should be served in all trades) maintain that it is unnecessary (the trade could be learnt in a much shorter time). The system encourages idleness on the part of the apprentice who, being unpaid, has no incentive to be otherwise. The passage again reflects Smith's conviction that the individual is the best judge of his own interest. "To judge whether he ["the workman"] is fit to be employed may surely be trusted to the discretion of the employers whose interest it so much concerns, The affected anxiety of the law giver lest they should employ an improper person is evidently as impertinent as it is oppressive."

By the abolition of apprenticeships "the public would be a gainer the work of all artificers in this way coming much cheaper to market." From this attack on apprenticeships Smith moves to a general attack on trade associations or, referring to the institutions of his time, "corporations" which exist, he says, "to prevent this reduction of price." Since such organisations are characteristic of towns he conducts a spirited defence of the countryside against the town. "In China and Indostan accordingly both the rank and the wages of country labourers are said to be superior to those of the greater part of artificers and manufacturers, they would probably be so everywhere if corporation laws and the corporation spirit did not prevent it." In particular he attacks any provisions, such as a register of those engaged in a particular trade, which encourage or facilitate "assemblies" for, in a famous sentence, "People of the same trade seldom meet together even for merriment and diversion, but the conversation ends in a conspiracy against the public or in some contrivance to raise prices."

He next attacks charitable educational provisions for those entering certain professions, notably the church and which, "draw many more people into those trades than could otherwise pretend to follow them." with the result that, "the long, tedious and expensive education . . . will not always procure them a suitable reward."

Lastly he attacks restrictions on mobility, both mobility between trades, which brings him back to the subject of apprenticeships and geographical mobility which leads him to attack certain contemporary English restrictions.

Productive and Unproductive Labour.

The next excerpt is perhaps the most vivid and polemical of Smith's arguments against state control and its tone goes a long way to explain its widespread political appeal. Although the distinction between productive and unproductive labour has been rejected by later economists the argument has an intuitive appeal which makes it easy to grasp: some labour has an end product and some does not.

". . . The labour of a manufacturer adds, generally, to the value of the materials he works upon, that of his own maintenance and of his master's profit. The labour of a menial servant on the contrary adds to the value of nothing." Those whose labour produces nothing include, "churchmen, lawyers, physicians, men of letters of all kinds; players, buffoons, musicians, opera-singers, opera-dancers, etc." Smith distinguishes between the part of annual produce which is used to "replace a capital" (in more contemporary jargon to recover outlay, or investment) and the part which constitutes "revenue" (a return over and above the original investment). The first must be spent on productive labour. - (This is a matter of logic. If nothing of value is produced nothing has been produced which can replace the capital) - The latter may be spent either on productive or on non-productive labour. He notes however a tendency to spend it on non-productive labour (or as would now more often be said, on consumption rather than investment). Smith goes on to make some comparisons between rich and poor countries (and historical periods). In poor countries and periods the proportion of annual produce used to replace capital will be much smaller since the capital concerned may consist of nothing but "a few wretched cattle." Again, in more modern terminology, this is to say that in such an economy there is little investment. There follow some rather moralistic passages. "The proportion between these different funds (ie: in the terms adopted here, investment and consumption) determines in every country the general character of the inhabitants as to industry or idleness." Some examples follow and he concludes, "Wherever capital predominates, industry prevails: wherever revenue, idleness" He spends several paragraphs amplifying the theme that, "Capitals are increased by parsimony, and diminished by prodigality and misconduct." and then comments, "Great nations are never impoverished by private, though they sometimes are by public prodigality and misconduct." and goes on to note that all those involved in government are unproductive. After observing that the continued increase in prosperity over centuries shows that "though the profusion of government must, undoubtedly, have retarded the natural progress of England towards wealth and improvement, it has not been able to stop it." This leads to a resounding passage. "It is the highest impertinence and presumption, therefore in kings and ministers, to pretend to watch over the economy of private people, and to restrain their expense... They are themselves always and without exception the greatest spendthrifts in the society." This sentence does not reaffirm but reflects his belief that individuals are the best judges of their own welfare.

Smith goes on to note that some forms of consumption ("expense") contribute more to "the growth of public opulence" than others. Durable goods can be accumulated and will eventually trickle down to bring a higher standard of living for the poor, "They are able to purchase them when their superiors grow weary of them, and the general accommodation of the whole people is thus gradually improved . . ." He concludes with an echo of his contention that self interest is the means to the general increase of wealth in society at large. Money spent on hospitality will be shared with others whereas expenditure on durable commodities will usually be purely selfish expenditure. This may indicate a base and selfish disposition but it will conduce more to "the growth of public opulence."

On Free Trade

Smith's chapter, *Of Restraints upon the Importation from Foreign Countries of such Goods as can be produced at Home* is a defence of free trade. It has been selected here both because of its stress on one of Smith's main themes, that individuals are better judges of their interest than public authorities and that the pursuit of private interest will itself secure the public interest. In particular the chapter contains the one place in the *Wealth of Nations* where Smith uses his famous phrase "invisible hand" ie: the mechanism by which the pursuit of individual interest achieves social benefit.

Smith begins by admitting that duty on imports encourages the development of the relevant home industry but questions whether this result is ultimately "more advantageous to the society". The argument continues with an assertion that the pursuit of private interest will secure the public interest. The point is, though Smith does not spell this out, that if the pursuit of private interest really does secure the interest of the wider society and if in certain circumstances individuals find it in their private interest to buy foreign goods then it must be in the interest of society to let them do so. First, he maintains, each individual will attempt to use his capital as near home as he can and therefore will invest it in home industries. Secondly, once he has done so, it will be in his interest to make the relevant home industry as profitable as possible. On this topic there appears the phrase "invisible hand." "By preferring the support of domestic to that of foreign industry; he intends only his own security; and by directing that industry in such a manner as its produce may be of the greatest value, he intends only his own gain, and he is in this, as in many other cases, led by an invisible hand to promote an end which was no part of his intention. Nor is it always the worse for the society that it was no part of it. By pursuing his own interest he frequently promotes that of the society more effectually than when he really intends to promote it."

After reiterating the better ability of the individual to judge his own interest Smith observes that to give a monopoly of the home market to domestic industry is "to direct private people in what way they ought to employ their capitals." (That is to say it prevents them from choosing to spend their money on foreign goods.) If the foreign produce is no cheaper than domestic produce the regulation must be "useless" otherwise it will be "hurtful." "It is the maxim of every prudent master of a family never to make at home what it will cost him more to make than to buy." What is prudence in the conduct of every private family can scarce be folly in that of a great kingdom."

Smith concedes that by means of protection a society may "acquire a particular manufacture" (develop a new industry) earlier than it would otherwise have done but points out that this fact does not guarantee that such a course of action will be of the greatest possible benefit to its economy.

He proceeds to some more concrete examples of the disadvantages of protection. In some cases it would obviously be absurd to attempt to avoid importation of foreign goods. Good wine could be produced in Scotland, but at thirty times the cost of imported wine. There follows a lengthy discussion of the importation of corn and cattle.

Smith goes on to concede two cases in which duties on imports may be acceptable. It may be that a particular industry should be protected because essential to the national defence. (He gives the example of the British Navigation Acts which gave certain privileges to domestic shipping thereby making it easier to maintain a navy.) It is also acceptable to impose duties on foreign goods where the same duties (and Smith insists this should mean strictly the same duties) are imposed on domestic goods. There are two further cases where the imposition of duties may be a matter for debate. It will be acceptable far a country to introduce duties as a retaliation against the imposition of duties on its own goods provided that such retaliation is directed strictly towards securing the removal of the initial duties and provided it is feasible to achieve this aim. It may also be acceptable to maintain duties on foreign goods where domestic industries have become dependent on these duties and their sudden removal might occasion "disorder." Smith notes, however, that such effects might be less than expected given the limited consequences of the entry into the labour market of soldiers and sailors at the conclusion of "the late war."

1. THE DIVISION OF LABOUR

The greatest improvement in the productive powers of labour, and the greater part of the skill, dexterity, and judgment with which it is anywhere directed, or applied, seem to have been the effects of the division of labour.

The effects of the division of labour, in the general business of society, will be more easily understood by considering in what manner it operates in some particular manufactures. It is commonly supposed to be carried furthest in some very trifling ones; not perhaps that it really is carried further in them than in others of more importance: but in those trifling manufactures which are destined to supply the small wants of but a small number of people, the whole number of workmen must necessarily be small; and those employed in every different branch of the work can often be collected into the same workhouse, and placed at once under the view of the spectator. In those great manufactures, on the contrary, which are destined to supply the great wants of the great body of the people, every different branch of the work employs so great a number of workmen that it is impossible to collect them all into the same workhouse. We can seldom see more, at one time, than those employed in one single branch. Though in such manufactures, therefore, the work may really be divided into a much greater number of parts than in those of a more trifling nature, the division is not near so obvious, and has accordingly been much less observed.

To take an example, therefore, from a very trifling manufacture; but one in which the division of labour has been very often taken notice of, the trade of the pin-maker; a workman not educated to this business (which the division of labour has rendered a distinct trade), nor acquainted with the use of the machinery employed in it (to the invention of which the same division of labour has probably given occasion), could scarce, perhaps, with his utmost industry, make one pin in a day, and certainly could not make twenty. But in the way in which this business is now carried on, not only the whole work is a peculiar trade, but it is divided into a number of branches, of which the greater part are likewise peculiar trades. One man draws out the wire, another straights it, a third cuts it, a fourth points it, a fifth grinds it at the top for receiving, the head; to make the head requires two or three distinct operations; to put it on is a peculiar business, to whiten the pins is another; it is even a trade by itself to put them into the paper; and the important business of making a pin is, in this manner, divided into about eighteen distinct operations, which, in some manufactories, are all performed by distinct hands, though in others the same man will sometimes perform two or three of them. I have seen a small manufactory of this kind where ten men only were employed, and where some of them consequently performed two or three distinct operations. But though they were very poor, and therefore but indifferently accommodated with the necessary machinery, they could, when they exerted themselves, make among them about twelve pounds of pins in a day. There are in a pound upwards of four thousand pins of a middling size. Those ten persons, therefore, could make among them upwards of forty-eight thousand pins in a day. Each person, therefore, making a tenth part of forty-eight thousand pins, might be considered as making four thousand eight hundred pins in a day. But if they had all wrought separately and independently, and without any of them having been educated to this peculiar business, they certainly could not each of them have made twenty, perhaps not one pin in a day; that is, certainly, not the two hundred and fortieth, perhaps not the four thousand eight hundredth part of what they are at present capable of performing, in consequence of a proper division and combination of their different operations.

In every other art and manufacture, the effects of the division of labour are similar to what they are in this very trifling one; though, in many of them, the labour can neither be so much subdivided, nor reduced to so great a simplicity of operation. The division of labour, however, so far as it can be introduced, occasions, in every art, a proportionable increase of the productive powers of labour. The separation of different trades and employments from one another seems to have taken place in consequence of this advantage. This separation, too, is generally called furthest in those countries which enjoy the highest degree of industry and improvement; what is the work of one man in a rude state of society being generally that of several in an improved one. In every improved society, the farmer is generally nothing but a farmer; the manufacturer, nothing but a manufacturer. The labour, too, which is necessary to produce any one complete manufacture is almost always divided among a great number of hands. How many different trades are employed in each branch of the linen and woollen manufactures from the growers of the flax and the wool, to the bleachers and smoothers of the linen, or to the dyers and dressers of the cloth! The nature of agriculture, indeed, does not admit of so many subdivisions of labour, nor of so complete a separation of one business from another, as manufactures. It is impossible to separate so entirely the business of the grazier from that of the corn-farmer as the trade of the carpenter is commonly separated from that of the smith. The spinner is almost always a distinct person from the weaver; but the ploughman, the harrower, the sower of the seed, and the reaper of the corn, are often the same. The occasions for those different sorts of labour returning with the different seasons of the year, it is impossible that one man should be constantly employed in any one of them. This impossibility of making so complete and entire a separation of all the different branches of labour employed in agriculture is perhaps the reason why the improvement of the productive powers of labour in this art does not always keep pace with their improvement in manufactures. The most opulent nations, indeed, generally excel all their neighbours in agriculture as well as in manufactures; but they are commonly more distinguished by their superiority in the latter than in the former. Their lands are in general better cultivated, and having more labour and expense bestowed upon them, produce more in proportion to the extent and natural fertility of the ground. But this superiority of produce is seldom much more than in proportion to the superiority of labour and expense. In agriculture, the labour of the rich country is not always much more productive than that of the poor; or, at least, it is never so much more productive as it commonly is in manufactures. The corn of the rich country, therefore, will not always, in the same degree of goodness, come cheaper to market than that of the poor. The corn of Poland, in the same degree of goodness, is as cheap as that of France, notwithstanding the superior opulence and improvement of the latter country. The corn of France is, in the corn provinces, fully as good, and in most years nearly about the same price with the corn of England, though, in opulence and improvement, France is perhaps inferior to England. The corn-lands of England, however, are better cultivated than those of France, and the corn-lands of France are said to be much better cultivated than those of Poland. But though the poor country, notwithstanding the inferiority of its cultivation, can, in some measure, rival the rich in the cheapness and goodness of its corn, it can pretend to no such competition in its manufactures; at least if those manufactures suit the soil, climate, and situation of the rich country. The silks of France are better and cheaper than those of England, because the silk manufacture, at least under the present high duties upon the importation of raw silk, does not so well suit the climate of England as that of France. But the hardware and the coarse woollens of England are beyond all comparison superior to those of France, and much cheaper too in the same degree of goodness. In Poland there are said to be scarce any manufactures of any kind, a few of those coarser household manufactures excepted, without which no country can well subsist.

This great increase of the quantity of work which, in consequence of the division of labour, the same number of people are capable of performing, is owing to three different circumstances; first, to the increase of dexterity in every particular workman; secondly, to the saving of the time which is commonly lost in passing from one species of work to another; and lastly, to the invention of a great number of machines which facilitate and abridge labour, and enable one man to do the work of many.

First, the improvement of the dexterity of the workman necessarily increases the quantity of the work he can perform; and the division of labour, by reducing every man's business to some one simple operation, and by making this operation the sole employment of his life, necessarily increased very much dexterity of the workman. A common smith, who, though accustomed to handle the hammer, has never been used to make nails, if upon some particular occasion he is obliged to attempt it, will scarce, I am assured, be able to make above two or three hundred nails in a day, and those too very bad ones. A smith who has been accustomed to make nails, but whose sole or principal business has not been that of a nailer, can seldom with his utmost diligence make more than eight hundred or a thousand nails in a day. I have seen several boys under twenty years of age who had never exercised any other trade but that of making nails, and who, when they exerted themselves, could make, each of them, upwards of two thousand three hundred nails in a day. The making of a nail, however, is by no means one of the simplest operations. The same person blows the bellows, stirs or mends the fire as there is occasion, heats the iron, and forges every part of the nail: in forging the head too he is obliged to change his tools. The different operations into which the making of a pin, or of a metal button, is subdivided, are all of them much more simple, and the dexterity of the person, of whose life it has been the sole business to perform them, is usually much greater. The rapidity with which some of the operations of those manufacturers are performed, exceeds what the human hand could, by those who had never seen them, be supposed capable of acquiring.

Secondly, the advantage which is gained by saving the time commonly lost in passing from one sort of work to another is much greater than we should at first view be apt to imagine it. It is impossible to pass very quickly from one kind of work to another that is carried on in a different place and with quite different tools. A country weaver, who cultivates a small farm, must lose a good deal of time in passing from his loom to the field, and from the field to his loom. When the two trades can be carried on in the same workhouse, the loss of time is no doubt much less. It is even in this case, however, very considerable. A man commonly saunters a little in turning his hand from one sort of employment to another. When he first begins the new work he is seldom very keen and hearty; his mind, as they say, does not go to it, and for some time he rather trifles than applies to good purpose. The habit of sauntering and of indolent careless application, which is naturally, or rather necessarily acquired by every country workman who is obliged to change his work and his tools every half hour, and to apply his hand in twenty different ways almost every day of his life, renders him almost always slothful and lazy, and incapable of any vigorous application even on the most pressing occasions. Independent, therefore, of his deficiency in point of dexterity, this cause alone must always reduce considerably the quantity of work which he is capable of performing.

Thirdly, and lastly, everybody must be sensible how much labour is facilitated and abridged by the application of proper machinery. It is unnecessary to give any example. I shall only observe, therefore, that the invention of all those machines by which labour is so much facilitated and abridged seems to have been originally owing to the division of labour. Men are much more likely to discover easier and readier methods of attaining any object when the whole attention of their minds is directed towards that single object than when it is dissipated among a great variety of things. But in consequence of the division of labour, the whole of every man's attention comes naturally to be directed towards some one very simple object. It is naturally to be expected, therefore, that some one or other of those who are employed in each particular branch of labour should soon find out easier and readier methods of performing their own particular work, wherever the nature of it admits of such improvement. A great part of the machines made use of in those manufactures in which labour is most subdivided, were originally the inventions of common workmen, who, being each of them employed in some very simple operation, naturally turned their thoughts towards finding out easier and readier methods of performing it. Whoever has been much accustomed to visit such manufactures must frequently have been shown very pretty machines, which were the inventions of such workmen in order to facilitate and quicken their particular part of the work. In the first fire-engines, a boy was constantly employed to open and shut alternately the communication between the boiler and the cylinder, according as the piston either ascended or descended. One of those boys, who loved to play with his companions, observed that, by tying a string from the handle of the valve which opened this communication to another part of the machine, the valve would open and shut without his assistance, and leave him at liberty to divert himself with his playfellows. One of the greatest improvements that has been made upon this machine, since it was first invented, was in this manner the discovery of a boy who wanted to save his own labour.

All the improvements in machinery, however, have by no means been the inventions of those who had occasion to use the machines. Many improvements have been made by the ingenuity of the makers of the machines, when to make them became the business of a peculiar trade; and some by that of those who are called philosophers or men of speculation, whose trade it is not to do anything, but to observe everything; and who, upon that account, are often capable of combining together the powers of the most distant and dissimilar objects. In the progress of society, philosophy or speculation becomes, like every other employment, the principal or sole trade and occupation of a particular class of citizens. Like every other employment too, it is subdivided into a great number of different branches, each of which affords occupation to a peculiar tribe or class of philosophers; and this subdivision of employment in philosophy, as well as in every other business, improves dexterity, and saves time. Each individual becomes more expert in his own peculiar branch, more work is done upon the whole, and the quantity of science is considerably increased by it.

It is the great multiplication of the productions of all the different arts, in consequence of the division of labour, which occasions, in a well-governed society, that universal opulence which extends itself to the lowest ranks of the people. Every workman has a great quantity of his own work to dispose of beyond what he himself has occasion for; and every other workman being exactly in the same situation, he is enabled to exchange a great quantity of his own goods for a great quantity, or, what comes to the same thing, for the price of a great quantity of theirs. He supplies them abundantly with what they have occasion for, and they accommodate him as amply with what he has occasion for, and a general plenty diffuses itself through all the different ranks of the society.

Observe the accommodation of the most common artificer or day-labourer in a civilised and thriving country, and you will perceive that the number of people of whose industry a part, though but a small part, has been employed in procuring him this accommodation, exceeds all computation. The woollen coat, for example, which covers the day-labourer, as coarse and rough as it may appear, is the produce of the joint labour of a great multitude of workmen. The shepherd, the sorter of the wool, the wool-comber or carder, the dyer, the scribbler, the spinner, the weaver, the fuller, the dresser, with many others, must all join their different arts in order to complete even this homely production. How many merchants and carriers, besides, must have been employed in transporting the materials from some of those workmen to others who often live in a very distant part of the country! How much commerce and navigation in particular, how many ship-builders, sailors, sail-makers, rope-makers, must have been employed in order to bring together the different drugs made use of by the dyer, which often come from the remotest corners of the world! What a variety of labour, too, is necessary in order to produce the tools of the meanest of those workmen! To say nothing of such complicated machines as the ship of the sailor, the mill of the fuller, or even the loom of the weaver, let us consider only what a variety of labour is requisite in order to form that very simple machine, the shears with which the shepherd clips the wool. The miner, the builder of the furnace for smelting the ore, the seller of the timber, the burner of the charcoal to be made use of in the smelting-house, the brickmaker, the brick-layer, the workmen who attend the furnace, the mill-wright, the forger, the smith, must all of them join their different arts in order to produce them. Were we to examine, in the same manner, all the different parts of his dress and household furniture, the coarse linen shirt which he wears next his skin, the shoes which cover his feet, the bed which he lies on, and all the different parts which compose it, the kitchen-grate at which he prepares his victuals, the coals which he makes use of for that purpose, dug from the bowels of the earth, and brought to him perhaps by a long sea and a long land carriage, all the other utensils of his kitchen, all the furniture of his table, the knives and forks, the earthen or pewter plates upon which he serves up and divides his victuals, the different hands employed in preparing his bread and his beer, the glass window which lets in the heat and the light, and keeps out the wind and the rain, with all the knowledge and art requisite for preparing that beautiful and happy invention, without which these northern parts of the world could scarce have afforded a very comfortable habitation, together with the tools of all the different workmen employed in producing those different conveniences; if we examine, I say, all these things, and consider what a variety of labour is employed about each of them, we shall be sensible that, without the assistance and co-operation of many thousands, the very meanest person in a civilised country could not be provided, even according to what we very falsely imagine the easy and simple manner in which he is commonly accommodated. Compared, indeed, with the more extravagant luxury of the great, his accommodation must no doubt appear extremely simple and easy; and yet it may be true, perhaps, that the accommodation of a European prince does not always so much exceed that of an industrious and frugal peasant as the accommodation of the latter exceeds that of many an African king, the absolute master of the lives and liberties of ten thousand naked savages.

This division of labour, from which so many advantages are derived, is not originally the effect of any human wisdom, which foresees and intends that general opulence to which it gives occasion. It is the necessary, though very slow and gradual consequence of a certain propensity in human nature which has in view no such extensive utility; the propensity to truck, barter, and exchange one thing for another.

Whether this propensity be one of those original principles in human nature of which no further account can be given; or whether, as seems more probable, it be the necessary consequence of the faculties of reason and speech, it belongs not to our present subject to inquire. It is common to all men, and to be found in no other race of animals, which seem to know neither this nor any other species of contracts. Two greyhounds, in running down the same hare, have sometimes the appearance of acting in some sort of concert. Each turns her towards his companion, or endeavours to intercept her when his companion turns her towards himself. This, however, is not the effect of any contract, but of the accidental concurrence of their passions in the same object at that particular time. Nobody ever saw a dog make a fair and deliberate exchange of one bone for another with another dog. Nobody ever saw one animal by its gestures and natural cries signify to another, this is mine, that yours; I am willing to give this for that. When an animal wants to obtain something either of a man or of another animal, it has no other means of persuasion but to gain the favour of those whose service it requires. A puppy fawns upon its dam, and a spaniel endeavours by a thousand attractions to engage the attention of its master who is at dinner, when it wants to be fed by him. Man sometimes uses the same arts with his brethren, and when he has no other means of engaging them to act according to his inclinations, endeavours by every servile and fawning attention to obtain their good will. He has not time, however, to do this upon every occasion. In civilised society he stands at all times in need of the cooperation and assistance of great multitudes, while his whole life is scarce sufficient to gain the friendship of a few persons. In almost every other race of animals each individual, when it is grown up to maturity, is entirely independent, and in its natural state has occasion for the assistance of no other living creature. But man has almost constant occasion for the help of his brethren, and it is in vain for him to expect it from their benevolence only. He will be more likely to prevail if he can interest their self-love in his favour, and show them that it is for their own advantage to do for him what he requires of them. Whoever offers to another a bargain of any kind, proposes to do this. Give me that which I want, and you shall have this which you want, is the meaning of every such offer; and it is in this manner that we obtain from one another the far greater part of those good offices which we stand in need of. It is not from the benevolence of the butcher, the brewer, or the baker that we expect our dinner, but from their regard to their own interest. We address ourselves, not to their humanity but to their self-love, and never talk to them of our own necessities but of their advantages. Nobody but a beggar chooses to depend chiefly upon the benevolence of his fellow-citizens. Even a beggar does not depend upon it entirely. The charity of well-disposed people, indeed, supplies him with the whole fund of his subsistence. But though this principle ultimately provides him with all the necessaries of life which he has occasion for, it neither does nor can provide him with them as he has occasion for them. The greater part of his occasional wants are supplied in the same manner as those of other people, by treaty, by barter, and by purchase. With the money which one man gives him he purchases food. The old clothes which another bestows upon him he exchanges for other old clothes which suit him better, or for lodging, or for food, or for money, with which he can buy either food, clothes, or lodging, as he has occasion.

As it is by treaty, by barter, and by purchase that we obtain from one another the greater part of those mutual good offices which we stand in need of, so it is this same trucking disposition which originally gives occasion to the division of labour. In a tribe of hunters or shepherds a particular person makes bows and arrows, for example, with more readiness and dexterity than any other. He frequently exchanges them for cattle or for venison with his companions; and he finds at last that he can in this manner get more cattle and venison than if he himself went to the field to catch them. From a regard to his own interest, therefore, the making of bows and arrows grows to be his chief business, and he becomes a sort of armourer. Another excels in making the frames and covers of their little huts or movable houses. He is accustomed to be of use in this way to his neighbours, who reward him in the same manner with cattle and with venison, till at last he finds it his interest to dedicate himself entirely to this employment, and to become a sort of house-carpenter. In the same manner a third becomes a smith or a brazier, a fourth a tanner or dresser of hides or skins, the principal part of the nothing of savages. And thus the certainty of being able to exchange all that surplus part of the produce of his own labour, which is over and above his own consumption, for such parts of the produce of other men's labour as he may have occasion for, encourages every man to apply himself to a particular occupation, and to cultivate and bring to perfection whatever talent or genius he may possess for that particular species of business.

The difference of natural talents in different men is, in reality, much less than we are aware of; and the very different genius which appears to distinguish men of different professions, when grown up to maturity, is not upon many occasions so much the cause as the effect of the division of labour. The difference between the most dissimilar characters, between a philosopher and a common street porter, for example, seems to arise not so much from nature as from habit, custom, and education. When they came into the world, and for the first six or eight years of their existence, they were perhaps very much alike, and neither their parents nor playfellows could perceive any remarkable difference. About that age, or soon after, they come to be employed in very different occupations. The difference of talents comes then to be taken notice of, and widens by degrees, till at last the vanity of the philosopher is willing to acknowledge scarce any resemblance. But without the disposition to truck, barter, and exchange, every man must have procured to himself every necessary and conveniency of life which he wanted. All must have had the same duties to perform, and the same work to do, and there could have been no such difference of employment as could alone give occasion to any great difference of talents.

As it is this disposition which forms that difference of talents, so remarkable among men of different professions, so it is this same disposition which renders that difference useful. Many tribes of animals acknowledged to be all of the same species derive from nature a much more remarkable distinction of genius, than what, antecedent to custom and education, appears to take place among men. By nature a philosopher is not in genius and disposition half so different from a street porter, as a mastiff is from a greyhound, or a greyhound from a spaniel, or this last from a shepherd's dog. Those different tribes of animals, however, though all of the same species, are of scarce any use to one another. The strength of the mastiff is not, in the least, supported either by the swiftness of the greyhound, or by the sagacity of the spaniel, or by the docility of the shepherd's dog. The effects of those different geniuses and talents, for want of the power or disposition to barter and exchange, cannot be brought into a common stock, and do not in the least contribute to the better accommodation ind conveniency of the species. Each animal is still obliged to support and defend itself, separately and independently, and derives no sort of advantage from that variety of talents with which nature has distinguished its fellows. Among men, on the contrary, the most dissimilar geniuses are of use to one another; the different produces of their respective talents, by the general disposition to truck, barter, and exchange, being brought, as it were, into a common stock, where every man may purchase whatever part of the produce of other men's talents he has occasion for.

'The Wealth of Nations,' Chapters 1 & 2

2. PROTECTION AND THE LABOUR MARKET

Such are the inequalities in the whole of advantages and disadvantages of the different employments of labour and stock, which the defect of any of the three requisites above mentioned must occasion, even where there is the most perfect liberty. But the policy of Europe, by not leaving things at perfect liberty, occasions other inequalities of much greater importance.

It does this chiefly in the three following ways. First, by restraining the competition in some employments to a smaller number than would otherwise be disposed to enter into them; secondly, by increasing it in others beyond what it naturally would be; and, thirdly, by obstructing the free circulation of labour and stock, both from employment to employment and from place to place.

First, the policy of Europe occasions a very important inequality in the whole of the advantages and disadvantages of the different employments of labour and stock, by restraining the competition in some employments to a smaller number than might otherwise be disposed to enter into them.

The exclusive privileges of corporations are the principal means it makes use of for this purpose.

The exclusive privilege of an incorporated trade necessarily restrains the competition, in the town where it is established, to those who are free of the trade. To have served an apprenticeship in the town, under a master properly qualified, is commonly the necessary requisite for obtaining this freedom. The bye laws of the corporation regulate sometimes the number of apprentices which any master is allowed to have, and almost always the number of years which each apprentice is obliged to serve. The intention of both regulations is to restrain the competition to a much smaller number than might otherwise be disposed to enter into the trade. The limitation of the number of apprentices restrains it directly. A long term of apprenticeship restrains it more indirectly, but as effectually, by increasing the expense of education.

In Sheffield no master cutler can have more than one apprentice at a time, by a bye law of the corporation. In Norfolk and Norwich no master weaver can have more than two apprentices, under pain of forfeiting five pounds a month to the king. No master hatter can have more than two apprentices anywhere in England, or in the English plantations, under pain of forfeiting five pounds a month, half to the king and half to him who shall sue in any court of record. Both these regulations, though they have been confirmed by a public law of the kingdom, are evidently dictated by the same corporation spirit which enacted the bye-law of Sheffield. The silk weavers in London had scarce been incorporated a year when they enacted a bye-law restraining any master from having more than two apprentices at a time. It required a particular Act of Parliament to rescind this bye law.

Seven years seem anciently to have been, all over Europe, the usual term established for the duration of apprenticeships in the greater part of incorporated trades. All such incorporations were anciently called universities, which indeed is the proper Latin name for any incorporation whatever. The university of smiths, the university of tailors, etc., are expressions which we commonly meet with in the old charters of ancient towns. When those particular incorporations which are now peculiarly called universities were first established, the term of years which it was necessary to study, in order to obtain the degree of master of arts, appears evidently to have been copied from the terms of apprenticeship in common trades, of which the incorporations were much more ancient. As to have wrought seven years under a master properly qualified was necessary in order to entitle any person to become a master, and to have himself apprenticed in a common trade; so to have studied seven years under a master properly qualified was necessary to entitle him to become a master, teacher, or doctor (words anciently synonymous) in the liberal arts, and to have scholars or apprentices (words likewise originally synonymous) to study under him.

By the 5th of Elizabeth, commonly called the Statute of Apprenticeship, it was enacted, that no person should for the future exercise any trade, craft, or mystery at that time exercised in England, unless he had previously served to it an apprenticeship of seven years at least; and what before had been the bye law of many particular corporations became in England the general and public law of all trades carried on in market towns. For though the words of the statute are very general, and seem plainly to include the whole kingdom, by interpretation its operation has been limited to market towns, it having been held that in country villages a person may exercise several different trades, though he has not served a seven years' apprenticeship to each, they being necessary for the conveniency of the inhabitants, and the number of people frequently not being sufficient to supply each with a particular set of hands.

By a strict interpretation of the words, too, the operation of this statute has been limited to those trades which were established in England before the 5th of Elizabeth, and has never been extended to such as have been introduced since that time. This limitation has given occasion to several distinctions which, considered as rules of police, appear as foolish as can well be imagined. It has been adjudged, for example, that a coachmaker can neither himself make nor employ journeymen to make his coach-wheels, but must buy them of a master wheel-wright; this latter trade having been exercised in England before the 5th of Elizabeth. But a wheelwright, though he has never served an apprenticeship to a coachmaker, may either himself make or employ journeyman to make coaches; the trade of a coachmaker not being within the statute, because not exercised in England at the time when it was made. The manufactures of Manchester, Birmingham, and Wolverhampton, are many of them, upon this account, not within the statute, not having been exercised in England before the 5th of Elizabeth.

In France, the duration of apprenticeships is different in different towns and in different trades. In Paris, five years is the term required in a great number; but before any person can be qualified to exercise the trade as a master, he must, in many of them, serve five years more as a journeyman. During this latter term he is called the companion of his master, and the term itself is called his companionship.

In Scotland there is no general law which regulates universally the duration of apprenticeships. The term is different in different corporations. Where it is long, a part of it may generally be redeemed by paying a small fine. In most towns, too, a very small fine is sufficient to purchase the freedom of any corporation. The weavers of linen and hempen cloth, the principal manufactures of the country, as well as all other artificers subservient to them, wheel-makers, reel-makers, etc., may exercise their trades in any town corporate without paying any fine. In all towns corporate all persons are free to sell butcher's meat upon any lawful day of the week. Three years in Scotland is a common term of apprenticeship, even in some very nice trades; and in general I know of no country in Europe in which corporation laws are so little oppressive.

The property which every man has in his own labour, as it is the original foundation of all other property, so it is the most sacred and inviolable. The patrimony of a poor man lies in the strength and dexterity of his hands; and to hinder him from employing this strength and dexterity of his hands; and to hinder him from employing this strength and dexterity in what manner he thinks proper without injury to his neighbour is a plain violation of this most sacred property. It is a manifest encroachment upon the just liberty both of the workman and of those who might be disposed to employ him. As it hinders the one from working at what he thinks proper, so it hinders the others from employing whom they think proper. To judge whether he is fit to be employed may surely be trusted to the discretion of the employers whose interest it so much concerns. The affected anxiety of the law-giver lest they should employ an improper person is evidently as impertinent as it is oppressive.

The institution of long apprenticeships can give no security that insufficient workmanship shall not frequently be exposed to public sale. When this is done it is generally the effect of fraud, and not of inability; and the longest apprenticeship can give no security against fraud. Quite different regulations are necessary to prevent this abuse. The sterling mark upon plate, and the stamps upon linen and woollen cloth, give the purchaser much greater security than any statute of apprenticeship. He generally looks at these, but never thinks it worth while to inquire whether the workman had served a seven years' apprenticeship.

The institution of long apprenticeships has no tendency to form a young people to industry. A journeyman who works by the piece is likely to be industrious, because he derives a benefit from every exertion of his industry. An apprentice is likely to be idle, and almost always is so, because he has no immediate interest to be otherwise. In the inferior employments, the sweets of labour consist altogether in the recompense of labour. They who are soonest in a condition to enjoy the sweets of it are likely soonest to conceive a relish for it, and to acquire the early habit of industry. A young man naturally conceives an aversion to labour when for a long time he receives no benefit from it. The boys who are put out apprentices from public charities are generally bound for more than the usual number of years, and they generally turn out very idle and worthless.

Apprenticeships were altogether unknown to the ancients. The reciprocal duties of master and apprentice make a considerable article in every modern code. The Roman law is perfectly silent with regard to them. I know no Greek or Latin word (I might venture, I believe, to assert that there is none) which expresses the idea we now annex to the word Apprentice, a servant bound to work at a particular trade for the benefit of a master, during a term of years, upon condition that the master shall teach him that trade.

Long apprenticeships are altogether unnecessary. The arts, which are much superior to common trades, such as those of making clocks and watches, contain no such mystery as to require a long course of instruction. The first invention of such beautiful machines, indeed, and even that of some of the instruments employed in making them, must, no doubt, have been the work of deep thought and long time, and may justly be considered as among the happiest efforts of human ingenuity. But when both have been fairly invented and are well understood, to explain to any young man, in the completest manner, how to apply the instruments and how to construct the machines, cannot well require more than the lessons of a few weeks: perhaps those of a few days might be sufficient. In the common mechanic trades, those of a few days might certainly be sufficient. The dexterity of hand, indeed, even in common trades, cannot be acquired without much practice and experience. But a young man would practice with much more diligence and attention, if from the beginning he wrought as a journeyman, being paid in proportion to the little work which he could execute, and paying in his turn for the materials which he might sometimes spoil through awkwardness and inexperience. His education would generally in this way be more effectual, and always less tedious and expensive. The master, indeed, would be a loser. He would lose all the wages of the apprentice, which he now saves, for seven years together. In the end, perhaps, the apprentice himself would be a loser. In a trade so easily learnt he would have more competitors, and his wages, when he came to be a complete workman, would be much less than at present. The same increase of competition would reduce the profits of the masters as well as the wages of the workmen. The trades, the crafts, the mysteries, would all be losers. But the public would be a gainer, the work of all artificers coming in this way much cheaper to market.

It is to prevent this reduction of price, and consequently of wages and profit, by restraining that free competition which would most certainly occasion it, that all corporations, and the greater part of corporation laws, have been established. In order to erect a corporation, no other authority in ancient times was requisite in many parts of Europe, but that of the town corporate in which it was established. In England, indeed, a charter from the king was likewise necessary. But this prerogative of the crown seems to have been reserved rather for extorting money from the subject than for the defence of the common liberty against such oppressive monopolies. Upon paying a fine to the king, the charter seems generally to have been readily granted; and when any particular class of artificers or traders thought proper to act as a corporation without a charter, such adulterine guilds, as they were called, were not always disfranchised upon that account, but obliged to fine annually to the king for permission to exercise their usurped privileges. The immediate inspection of all corporations, and of the bye-laws which they might think proper to enact for their own government, belonged to the town corporate in which they were established; and whatever discipline was exercised over them proceeded commonly, not from the king, but from the greater incorporation of which those subordinate ones were only parts or members.

The government of towns corporate was altogether in the hands of traders and artificers, and it was the manifest interest of every particular class of them to prevent the market from being overstocked, as they commonly express it, with their own particular species of industry, which is in reality to keep it always understocked. Each class was eager to establish regulations proper for this purpose, and, provided it was allowed to do so, was willing to consent that every other class should do the same. In consequence of such regulations, indeed, each class was obliged to buy the goods they had occasion for from every other within the town, somewhat dearer than they otherwise might have done. But in recompense, they were enabled to sell their own just as much dearer; so that so far it was as broad as long, as they say; and in the dealings of the different classes within the town with one another, none of them were losers by these regulations. But in their dealings with the country they were all great gainers; and in these latter dealings consists the whole trade which supports and enriches every town.

Every town draws its whole subsistence, and all the materials of its industry, from the country. It pays for these chiefly in two ways: first, by sending back to the country a part of those materials wrought up and manufactured; in which case their price is augmented by the wages of the workmen, and the profits of their masters or immediate employers; secondly, by sending to it a part both of the rude and manufactured produce, either of other countries, or of distant parts of the same country, imported into the town; in which case, too, the original price of those goods is augmented by the wages of the carriers or sailors, and by the profits of the merchants who employ them. In what is gained upon the first of those two branches of commerce consists the advantage which the town makes by its manufactures; in what is gained upon the second, the advantage of its inland and foreign trade. The wages of the workmen, and the profits of their different employers, make up the whole of what is gained upon both. Whatever regulations, therefore, tend to increase those wages and profits beyond what they otherwise would be, tend to enable the town to purchase, with a smaller quantity of its labour, the produce of a greater quantity of the labour of the country. They give the traders and artificers in the town an advantage over the landlords, farmers, and labourers in the country, and break down that natural equality which would otherwise take place in the commerce which is carried on between them. The whole annual produce of the labour of the society is annually divided between those two different sets of people. By means of those regulations a greater share of it is given to the inhabitants of the town than would otherwise fall to them; and a less to those of the country.

The price which the town really pays for the provisions and materials annually imported into it is the quantity of manufactures and other goods annually exported from it. The dearer the latter are sold, the cheaper the former are bought. The industry of the town becomes more, and that of the country less advantageous.

That the industry which is carried on in towns is, everywhere in Europe, more advantageous than that which is carried on in the country, without entering into any very nice computations, we may satisfy ourselves by one very simple and obvious observation. In every country of Europe we find, at least, a hundred people who have acquired great fortunes from small beginnings by trade and manufactures, the industry which properly belongs to towns, for one who has done so by that which properly belongs to the country, the raising of rude produce by the improvement and cultivation of land. Industry, therefore, must be better rewarded, the wages of labour and the profits of stock must evidently be greater in the one situation than in the other. But stock and labour naturally seek the most advantageous employment. They naturally, therefore, resort as much as they can to the town, and desert the country.

The inhabitants of a town, being collected into one place, can easily combine together. The most insignificant trades carried on in towns have accordingly, in some place or other, been incorporated, and even where they have never been incorporated, yet the corporation spirit, the jealousy of strangers, the aversion to take apprentices, or to communicate the secret of their trade, generally prevail in them, and often teach them, by voluntary associations and agreements, to prevent that free competition which they cannot prohibit by bye-laws. The trades which employ but a small number of hands run most easily into such combinations. Half a dozen wool-combers, perhaps, are necessary to keep a thousand spinners and weavers at work. By combining not to take apprentices they can not only engross the employment, but reduce the whole manufacture into a sort of slavery to themselves, and raise the price of their labour much above what is due to the nature of their work.

The inhabitants of the country, dispersed in distant places, cannot easily combine together. They have not only never been incorporated, but the corporation spirit never has prevailed among them. No apprenticeship has ever been thought necessary to qualify for husbandry, the great trade of the country. After what are called the fine arts, and the liberal professions, however, there is perhaps no trade which requires so great a variety of knowledge and experience. The innumerable volumes which have been written upon it in all languages may satisfy us that, among the wisest and most learned nations, it has never been regarded as a matter very easily understood. And from all those volumes we shall in vain attempt to collect that knowledge of its various and complicated operations, which is commonly possessed even by the common farmer; how contemptuously soever the very contemptible authors of some of them may sometimes affect to speak of him. There is scarce any common mechanic trade, on the contrary, of which all the operations may not be as completely and distinctly explained in a pamphlet of a very few pages, as it is possible for words illustrated by figures to explain them. In the history of the arts, now publishing by the French Academy of Sciences, several of them are actually explained in this manner. The direction of operations, besides, which must be varied with every change of the weather, as well as with many other accidents, requires much more judgment and discretion than that of those which are always the same or very nearly the same.

Not only the art of the farmer, the general direction of the operations of husbandry, but many inferior branches of country labour require much more skin and experience than the greater part of mechanic trades. The man who works upon brass and iron, works with instruments and upon materials of which the temper is always the same, or very nearly the same. But the man who ploughs the ground with a team of horses or oxen, works with instruments of which the health, strength, and temper, are very different upon different occasions. The condition of the materials which he works upon, too, is as variable as that of the instruments which he works with, and both require to be managed with much judgment and discretion. The common ploughman, though generally regarded as the pattern of stupidity and ignorance, is seldom defective in this judgment and discretion. He is less accustomed, indeed, to social intercourse than the mechanic who lives in a town. His voice and language are more uncouth and more difficult to be understood by those who are not used to them. His understanding, however, being accustomed to consider a greater variety of objects, is generally much superior to that of the other, whose whole attention from morning till night is commonly occupied in performing one or two very simple operations. How much the lower ranks of people in the country are really superior to those of the town is well known to every man whom either business or curiosity has led to converse much with both. In China and Indostan accordingly both the rank and the wages of country labourers are said to be superior to those of the greater part of artificers and manufacturers. They would probably be so everywhere, if corporation laws and the corporation spirit did not prevent it.

The superiority which the industry of the towns has everywhere in Europe over that of the country is not altogether owing to corporations and corporation laws. It is supported by many other regulations. The high duties upon foreign manufactures and upon all goods imported by alien merchants, all tend to the same purpose. Corporation laws enable the inhabitants of towns to raise their prices, without fearing to be undersold by the free competition of their own countrymen. Those other regulations secure them equally against that of foreigners. The enhancement of price occasioned by both is everywhere finally paid by the landlords, farmers, and labourers of the country, who have seldom opposed the establishment of such monopolies. They have commonly neither inclination nor fitness to enter into combinations; and the clamour and sophistry of merchants and manufacturers easily persuade them that the private interest of a part, and of a subordinate part of the society, is the general interest of the whole.

In Great Britain the superiority of the industry of the towns over that of the country seems to have been greater formerly than in the present times. The wages of country labour approach nearer to those of manufacturing labour, and the profits of stock employed in agriculture to those of trading and manufacturing stock, than they are said to have done in the last century, or in the beginning of the present. This change may be regarded as the necessary, though very late consequence of the extraordinary encouragement given to the industry of the towns. The stock accumulated in them comes in time to be so great that it can no longer be employed with the ancient profit in that species of industry which is peculiar to them. That industry has its limits like every other; and the increase of stock, by increasing the competition, necessarily reduces the profit. The lowering of profit in the town forces out stock to the country, where, by creating a new demand for country labour, it necessarily raises its wages. It then spreads itself, if I may say so, over the face of the land, and by being employed in agriculture is in part restored to the country, at the expense of which, in a great measure, it had originally been accumulated in the town. That everywhere in Europe the greatest improvements of the country have been owing to such overflowings of the stock originally accumulated in the towns, I shall endeavour to show hereafter; and at the same time to demonstrate that, though some countries have by this course attained to a considerable degree of opulence, it is in itself necessarily slow, uncertain, liable to be disturbed and interrupted by innumerable accidents, and in every respect contrary to the order of nature and of reason. The interests, prejudices, laws and customs, which have given occasion to it, I shall endeavour to explain as fully and distinctly as I can in the third and fourth books of this Inquiry.

People of the same trade seldom meet together, even for merriment and diversion, but the conversation ends in a conspiracy against the public, or in some contrivance to raise prices. It is impossible indeed to prevent such meetings, by any law which either could be executed, or would be consistent with liberty and justice. But though the law cannot hinder people of the same trade from sometimes assembling together, it ought to do nothing to facilitate such assemblies, much less to render them necessary.

A regulation which obliges all those of the same trade in a particular town to enter their names and places of abode in a public register, facilitates such assemblies. It connects individuals who might never otherwise be known to one another, and gives every man of the trade a direction where to find every other man of it.

A regulation which enables those of the same trade to tax themselves in order to provide for their poor, their sick, their widows and orphans, by giving them a common interest to manage, renders such assemblies necessary.

An incorporation not only renders them necessary, but makes the act of the majority binding upon the whole. In a free trade an effectual combination cannot be established but by the unanimous consent of every single trader, and it cannot last longer than every single trader continues of the same mind. The majority of a corporation can enact a bye-law with proper penalties, which will limit the competition more effectually and more durably than any voluntary combination whatever.

The pretence that corporations are necessary for the better government of the trade is without any foundation. The real and effectual discipline which is exercised over a workman is not that of his corporation, but that of his customers. It is the fear of losing their employment which restrains his frauds and corrects his negligence. An exclusive corporation necessarily weakens the force of this discipline. A particular set of workmen must then be employed, let them behave well or ill. It is upon this account that in many large incorporated towns no tolerable workmen are to be found, even in some of the most necessary trades. If you would have your work tolerably executed, it must be done in the suburbs, where the workmen, having no exclusive privilege, have nothing but their character to depend upon, and you must then smuggle it into the town as well as you can.

It is in this manner that the policy of Europe, by restraining the competition in some employments to a smaller number than would otherwise be disposed to enter into them, occasions a very important inequality in the whole of the advantages and disadvantages of the different employments of labour and stock.

Secondly, the policy of Europe, by increasing the competition in some employments beyond what it naturally would be, occasions another inequality of an opposite kind in the whole of the advantages and disadvantages of the different employments of labour and stock.

It has been considered as of so much importance that a proper number of young people should be educated for certain professions, that sometimes the public and sometimes the piety of private founders have established many pensions, scholarships, exhibitions, bursaries, etc., for this purpose, which draw many more people into those trades than could otherwise pretend to follow them. In all Christian countries, I believe, the education of the greater part of churchmen is paid for in this manner. Very few of them are educated altogether at their own expense. The long, tedious, and expensive education, therefore, of those who are, will not always procure them a suitable reward, the church being crowded with people who, in order to get employment, are willing to accept of a much smaller recompense than what such an education would otherwise have entitled them to; and in this manner the competition of the poor takes away the reward of the rich. It would be indecent, no doubt, to compare either a curate or a chaplain with a journeyman in any common trade. The pay of a curate or chaplain, however, may very properly be considered as of the same nature with the wages of a journeyman. They are, all three, paid for their work according to the contract which they may happen to make with their respective superiors. Till after the middle of the fourteenth century, five merks, containing about as much silver as ten pounds of our present money, was in England the usual pay of a curate or a stipendiary parish priest, as we find it regulated by the decrees of several different national councils. At the same period fourpence a day, containing the same quantity of silver as a shilling of our present money, was declared to be the pay of a master mason, and threepence a day, equal to ninepence of our present money, that of a journeyman mason. The wages of both these labourers, therefore, supposing them to have been constantly employed, were much superior to those of the curate. The wages of the master mason, supposing him to have been without employment one third of the year, would have fully equalled them. By the 12th of Queen Anne, c. 12, it is declared, "That whereas for want of sufficient maintenance and encouragement to curates, the cures have in several places been meanly supplied, the bishop is, therefore, empowered to appoint by writing under his band and seal a sufficient certain stipend or allowance, not exceeding fifty and not less than twenty pounds a year." Forty pounds a year is reckoned at present very good pay for a curate, and notwithstanding this Act of Parliament there are many curacies under twenty pounds a year. There are journeymen shoemakers in London who earn forty pounds a year, and there is scarce an industrious workman of any kind in that metropolis who does not earn more than twenty. This last sum indeed does not exceed what is frequently earned by common labourers in many country parishes. Whenever the law has attempted to regulate the wages of workmen, it has always been rather to lower them than to raise them. But the law has upon many occasions attempted to raise the wages of curates, and for the dignity of the church, to oblige the rectors of parishes to give them more than the wretched maintenance which they themselves might be willing to accept of. And in both cases the law seems to have been equally ineffectual, and has never either been able to raise the wages of curates, or to sink those of labourers to the degree that was intended; because it has never been able to hinder either the one from being willing to accept of less than the legal allowance, on account of the indigence of their situation and the multitude of their competitors; or the other from receiving more, on account of the contrary competition of those who expected to derive either profit or pleasure from employing them.

The great benefices and other ecclesiastical dignities support the honour of the church, notwithstanding the mean circumstance of some of its inferior members. The respect paid to the profession, too, makes some compensation even to them for the meanness of their pecuniary recompense. In England, and in all Roman Catholic countries, the lottery of the church is in reality much more advantageous than is necessary. The example of the churches of Scotland, of Geneva, and of several other Protestant churches, may satisfy us that in so creditable a profession, in which education is so easily procured, the hopes of much more moderate benefices will draw a sufficient number of learned, decent, and respectable men into holy orders.

In professions in which there are no benefices, such as law and physic, if an equal proportion of people were educated at the public expense, the competition would soon be so great as to sink very much their pecuniary reward. It might then not be worth any man's while to educate his son to either of those professions at his own expense. They would be entirely abandoned to such as had been educated by those public charities, whose numbers and necessities would oblige them in general to content themselves with a very miserable recompense, to the entire degradation of the now respectable professions of law and physic.

That unprosperous race of men commonly called men of letters are pretty much in the situation which lawyers and physicians probably would be in upon the foregoing supposition. In every part of Europe the greater part of them have been educated for the church, but have been hindered by different reasons from entering into holy orders. They have generally, therefore, been educated at the public expense, and their numbers are everywhere so great as commonly to reduce the price of their labour to a very paltry recompense.

Before the invention of the art of printing, the only employment by which a man of letters could make anything by his talents was that of a public or private teacher, or by communicating to other people the curious and useful knowledge which he had acquired himself: and this is still surely a more honourable, a more useful, and in general even a more profitable employment than that other of writing for a bookseller, to which the art of printing has given occasion. The time and study, the genius, knowledge, and application requisite to qualify an eminent teacher of the sciences, are at least equal to what is necessary for the greatest practitioners in law and physic. But the usual reward of the eminent teacher bears no proportion to that of the lawyer or physician; because the trade of the one is crowded with indigent people who have been brought up to it at the public expense; whereas those of the other two are encumbered with very few who have not been educated at their own. The usual recompense, however, of public and private teachers, small as it may appear, would undoubtedly be less than it is, if the competition of those yet more indigent men of letters who write for bread was not taken out of the market. Before the invention of the art of printing, a scholar and a beggar seem to have been terms very nearly synonymous. The different governors of the universities before that time appear to have often granted licences to their scholars to beg.

In ancient times, before any charities of this kind had been established for the education of indigent people to the learned professions, the rewards of eminent teachers appear to have been much more considerable. Isocrates, in what is called his discourse against the sophists, reproaches the teachers of his own times with inconsistency. "They make the most magnificent promises to their scholars," says he, "and undertake to teach them to be wise, to be happy, and to be just, and in return for so important a service they stipulate the paltry reward of four or five minae. They who teach wisdom," continues he, "ought certainly to be wise themselves; but if any man were to sell such a bargain for such a price, he would be convicted of the most evident folly." He certainly does not mean here to exaggerate the reward, and we may be assured that it was not less than he represents it. Four minae were equal to thirteen pounds six shillings and eightpence: five minae to sixteen pounds thirteen shillings and fourpence. Something not less than the largest of those two sums, therefore, must at that time have been usually paid to the most eminent teachers at Athens. Isocrates himself demanded ten minae, or thirty-three pounds six shillings and eightpence, from each scholar. When he taught at Athens, he is said to have had a hundred scholars. I understand this to be the number whom he taught at one time, or who attended what we could call one course of lectures, a number which will not appear extraordinary from so great a city to so famous a teacher, who taught, too, what was at that time the most fashionable of all sciences, rhetoric. He must have made, therefore, by each course of lectures, a thousand minae, or £3333 6s. 8d. A thousand minae, accordingly, is said by Plutarch in another place, to have been his Didactron, or usual price of teaching. Many other eminent teachers in those times appear to have acquired great fortunes. Gorgias made a present to the temple of Delphi of his own statue in solid gold. We must not, I presume, suppose that it was as large as the life. His way of living, as well as that of Hippias and Protagoras, two other eminent teachers of those times, is represented by Plato as splendid even to ostentation. Plato himself is said to have lived with a good deal of magnificence. Aristotle, after having been tutor to Alexander, and most munificently rewarded, as it is universally agreed, both by him and his father Philip, thought it worth while, notwithstanding, to return to Athens, in order to resume the teaching of his school. Teachers of the sciences were probably in those times less common than they came to be in an age or two afterwards, when the competition had probably somewhat reduced both the price of their labour and the admiration for their persons. The most eminent of them, however, appear always to have enjoyed a degree of consideration much superior to any of the like profession in the present times. The Athenians sent Carneades the Academic, and Diogenes the Stoic, upon a solemn embassy to Rome; and though their city had then declined from its former grandeur, it was still an independent and considerable republic. Carneades, too, was a Babylonian by birth, and as there never was a people more jealous of admitting foreigners to public offices than the Athenians, their consideration for him must have been very great.

This inequality is upon the whole, perhaps, rather advantageous than hurtful to the public. It may somewhat degrade the profession of a public teacher; but the cheapness of literary education is surely an advantage which greatly overbalances this trifling inconveniency. The public, too, might derive still greater benefit from it, if the constitution of those schools and colleges, in which education is carried on, was more reasonable than it is at present through the greater part of Europe.

Thirdly, the policy of Europe, by obstructing the free circulation of labour and stock both from employment to employment, and from place to place, occasions in some cases a very incovenient inequality in the whole of the advantages and disadvantages of their different employments.

The Statute of Apprenticeship obstructs the free circulation of labour from one employment to another, even in the same place. The exclusive privileges of corporations obstruct it from one place to another, even in the same employment.

It frequently happens that while high wages are given to the workmen in one manufacture, those in another are obliged to content themselves with bare subsistence. The one is in an advancing state, and has, therefore, a continual demand for new bands: the other is in a declining state, and the superabundance of hands is continually increasing. Those two manufactures may sometimes be in the same town, and sometimes in the same neighbourhood, without being able to lend the least assistance to one another. The Statute of Apprenticeship may oppose it in the one case, and both that and an exclusive corporation in the other. In many different manufactures, however, the operations are so much alike, that the workmen could easily change trades with one another, if those absurd laws did not hinder them. The arts of weaving plain linen and plain silk, for example, are almost entirely the same. That of weaving plain woollen is somewhat different; but the difference is so insignificant that either a linen or a silk weaver might become a tolerable work in a very few days. If any of those three capital manufactures, therefore, were decaying, the workmen might find a resource in one of the other two which was in a more prosperous condition; and their wages would neither rise too high in the thriving, nor sink too low in the decaying manufacture. The linen manufacture indeed is, in England, by a particular statute, open to everybody; but as it is not much cultivated through the greater part of the country, it can afford no general resource to the workmen of other decaying manufactures, who, wherever the Statute of Apprenticeship takes place, have no other choice but either to come upon the parish, or to work as common labourers, for which, by their habits, they are much worse qualified than for any sort of manufacture that bears any resemblance to their own. They generally, therefore, choose to come upon the parish.

Whatever obstructs the free circulation of labour from one employment to another obstructs that of stock likewise; the quantity of stock which can be employed in any branch of business depending very much upon that of the labour which can be employed in it. Corporation laws, however, give less obstruction to the free circulation of stock from one place to another than to that of labour. It is everywhere much easier for a wealthy merchant to obtain the privilege of trading in a town corporate, than for a poor artificer to obtain that of working in it.

The obstruction which corporation laws give to the free circulation of labour is common, I believe, to every part of Europe. That which is given to it by the Poor Laws is, so far as I know, peculiar to England. It consists in the difficulty which a poor man finds in obtaining a settlement, or even in being allowed to exercise his industry in any parish but that to which he belongs. It is the labour of artificers and manufacturers only of which the free circulation is obstructed by corporation laws. The difficulty of obtaining settlements obstructs even that of common labour. It may be worth while to give some account of the rise, progress, and present state of this disorder, the greatest perhaps of any in the police of England.

When by the destruction of monasteries the poor had been deprived of the charity of those religious houses, after some other ineffectual attempts for their relief, it was enacted by the 43rd of Elizabeth, c. 2, that every parish should be bound to provide for its own poor; and that overseers of the poor should be annually appointed, who, with the churchwardens, should raise by a parish rate competent sums for this purpose.

By this statute the necessity of providing for their own poor was indispensably imposed upon every parish. Who were to be considered as the poor of each parish became, therefore, a question of some importance. This question, after some variation, was at last determined by the 13th and 14th of Charles II when it was enacted, that forty days' undisturbed residence should gain any person a settlement in any parish; but that within that time it should be lawful for two justices of the peace, upon complaint made by the churchwardens or overseers of the poor, to remove any new inhabitant to the parish where he was last legally settled; unless he either rented a tenement of ten pounds a year, or could give such security for the discharge of the parish where he was then living, as those justices should judge sufficient.

Some frauds, it is said, were committed in consequence of this statute; parish officers sometimes bribing their own poor to go clandestinely to another parish, and by keeping themselves concealed for forty days to gain a settlement there, to the discharge of that to which they properly belonged. It was enacted, therefore, by the 1st of James II that the forty days' undisturbed residence of any person necessary to gain a settlement should be accounted only from the time of his delivering notice in writing, of the place of his abode and the number of his family, to one of the churchwardens or overseers of the parish where he came to dwell.

But parish officers, it seems, were not always more honest with regard to their own, than they had been with regard to other parishes, and sometimes connived at such intrusions, receiving the notice, and taking no proper steps in consequence of it. As every person in a parish, therefore, was supposed to have an interest to prevent as much as possible their being burdened by such intruders, it was further enacted by the 3rd of William III that the forty days' residence should be accounted only from the publication of such notice in writing on Sunday in the church, immediately after divine service.

"After all," says Doctor Burn, "this kind of settlement, by continuing forty days after publication of notice in writing, is very seldom obtained; and the design of the acts is not so much for gaining of settlements, as for the avoiding of them, by persons coming into a parish clandestinely: for the giving of notice is only putting a force upon the parish to remove. But if a person's situation is such, that it is doubtful whether he is actually removable or not, he shall by giving of notice compel the parish either to allow him a settlement uncontested, by suffering him to continue forty days; or, by removing him, to try the right."

This statute, therefore, rendered it almost impracticable for a poor man to gain a new settlement in the old way, by forty days' inhabitancy. But that it might not appear to preclude altogether the common people of one parish from ever establishing themselves with security in another, it appointed four other ways by which a settlement might be gained without any notice delivered or published. The first was, by being taxed to parish rates and paying them; the second, by being elected into an annual parish office, and serving in it a year; the third, by serving an apprenticeship in the parish; the fourth, by being hired into service there for a year, and continuing in the same service during the whole of it.

Nobody can gain a settlement by either of the two first ways, but by the public deed of the whole parish, who are too well aware of the consequences to adopt any new-comer who has nothing but his labour to support him, either by taxing him to parish rates, or by electing him into a parish office.

No married man can well gain any settlement in either of the two last ways. An apprentice is scarce ever married; and it is expressly enacted that no married servant shall gain any settlement by being hired for a year. The principal effect of introducing settlement by service has been to put out in a great measure the old fashion of hiring for a year, which before had been so customary in England, that even at this day, if no particular term is agreed upon, the law intends that every servant is hired for a year. But masters are not always willing to give their servants a settlement by hiring them in this manner; and servants are not always willing to be so hired, because, as every last settlement discharges all the foregoing, they might thereby lose their original settlement in the places of their nativity, the habitation of their parents and relations.

No independent workman, it is evident, whether labourer or artificer, is likely to gain any new settlement either by apprenticeship or by service. When such a person, therefore, carried his industry to a new parish, he was liable to be removed, how healthy and industrious soever, at the caprice of any churchwarden or overseer, unless he either rented a tenement of ten pounds a year, a thing impossible for one who has nothing but his labour to live by; or could give such security for the discharge of the parish as two justices of the peace should judge sufficient. What security they shall require, indeed, is left altogether to their discretion; but they cannot well require less than thirty pounds, it having been enacted that the purchase even of a freehold estate of less than thirty pounds' value shall not gain any person a settlement, as not being sufficient for the discharge of the parish. But this is a security which scarce any man who lives by labour can give; and much greater security is frequently demanded.

In order to restore in some measure that free circulation of labour which those different statutes had almost entirely taken away, the invention of certificates was fallen upon. By the 8th and 9th of William III it was enacted that if any person should bring a certificate from the parish where he was last legally settled, subscribed by the churchwardens and overseers of the poor, and allowed by two justices of the peace, that every other parish should be obliged to receive him; that he should not be removable merely upon account of his being likely to become chargeable, but only upon his becoming actually chargeable, and that then the parish which granted the certificate should be obliged to pay the expense both of his maintenance and of his removal. And in order to give the most perfect security to the parish where such certificated man should come to reside, it was further enacted by the same statute that he should gain no settlement there by any means whatever, except either by renting a tenement of ten pounds a year, or by serving upon his own account in an annual parish office for one whole year; and consequently neither by notice, nor by service, nor by apprenticeship, nor by paying parish rates. By the 12th of Queen Anne, too, stat. 1, c. 18, it was further enacted that neither the servants nor apprentices of such certificated man should gain any settlement in the parish where he resided under such certificate.

How far this invention has restored that free circulation of labour which the preceding statutes had almost entirely taken away, we may learn from the following very judicious observation of Doctor Burn. "It is obvious," says he, "that there are divers good reasons for requiring certificates with persons coming to settle in any place; namely, that persons residing under them can gain no settlement, neither by apprenticeship, nor by service, nor by giving notice, nor by paying parish rates; that they can settle neither apprentices nor servants; that if they become chargeable, it is certainly known whither to remove them, and the parish shall be paid for the removal, and for their maintenance in the meantime; and that if they fall sick, and cannot be removed, the parish which gave the certificate must maintain them: none of all which can be without a certificate. Which reasons will hold proportionably for parishes not granting certificates in ordinary cases; for it is far more than an equal chance, but that they will have the certificated persons again, and in a worse condition." The moral of this observation seems to be that certificates ought always to be required by the parish where any poor man comes to reside, and that they ought very seldom to be granted by that which he proposes to leave. "There is somewhat of hardship in this matter of certificates," says the same very intelligent author in his History of the Poor Laws, "by putting it in the power of a parish officer to imprison a man as it were for life; however inconvenient it may be for him to continue at that place where he has had the misfortune to acquire what is called a settlement, or whatever advantage he may propose to himself by living elsewhere."

Though a certificate carries along with it no testimonial of good behaviour, and certifies nothing but that the person belongs to the parish to which he really does belong, it is altogether discretionary in the parish officers either to grant or to refuse it. A mandamus was once moved for, says Doctor Burn, to compel the churchwardens and overseers to sign a certificate; but the court of King's Bench rejected the motion as a very strange attempt.

The very unequal price of labour which we frequently find in England in places at no great distance from one another is probably owing to the obstruction which the law of settlements gives to a poor man who would carry his industry from one parish to another without a certificate. A single man, indeed, who is healthy and industrious, may sometimes reside by sufferance without one; but a man with a wife and family who should attempt to do so would in most parishes be sure of being removed, and if the single man should afterwards marry, he would generally be removed likewise. The scarcity of hands in one parish, therefore, cannot always be relieved by their superabundance in another, as it is constantly in Scotland, and, I believe, in all other countries where there is no difficulty of settlement. In such countries, though wages may sometimes rise a little in the neighbourhood of a great town, or wherever else there is an extraordinary demand for labour, and sink gradually as the distance from such places increases, till they fall back to the common rate of the country; yet we never meet with those sudden and unaccountable differences in the wages of neighbouring places which we sometimes find in England, where it is often more difficult for a poor man to pass the artificial boundary of a parish than an arm of the sea or a ridge of high mountains, natural boundaries which sometimes separate very distinctly different rates of wages in other countries.

To remove a man who has committed no misdemeanour from the parish where he chooses to reside is an evident violation of natural liberty and justice. The common people of England, however, so jealous of their liberty, but like the common people of most other countries never rightly understanding wherein it consists, have now for more than a century together suffered themselves to be exposed to this oppression without a remedy. Though men of reflection, too, have sometimes complained of the law of settlements as a public grievance; yet it has never been the object of any general popular clamour, such as that against general warrants, an abusive practice undoubtedly, but such a one as was not likely to occasion any general oppression. There is scarce a poor man in England of forty years of age, I will venture to say, who has not in some part of his life felt himself most cruelly oppressed by this ill contrived law of settlements.

I shall conclude this long chapter with observing that, though anciently it was usual to rate wages, first by general laws extending over the whole kingdom, and afterwards by particular orders of the justices of peace in every particular county, both these practices have now gone entirely into disuse. "By the experience of above four hundred years," says Doctor Burn, "it seems time to lay aside all endeavours to bring under strict regulations, what in its own nature seems incapable of minute limitation; for if all persons in the same kind of work were to receive equal wages, there would be no emulation, and no room left for industry or ingenuity."

Particular Acts of Parliament, however, still attempt sometimes to regulate wages in particular trades and in particular places. Thus the 8th of George III prohibits under heavy penalties all master tailors in London, and five miles round it, from giving, and their workmen from accepting, more than two shillings and sevenpence halfpenny a day, except in the case of a general mourning. Whenever the legislature attempts to regulate the differences between masters and their workmen, its counsellors are always the masters. When the regulation, therefore, is in favour of the workmen, it is always just and equitable; but it is sometimes otherwise when in favour of the masters. Thus the law which obliges the masters in several different trades to pay their workmen in money and not in goods is quite just and equitable. It imposes no real hardship upon the masters. It only obliges them to pay that value in money, which they pretended to pay, but did not always really pay, in goods. This law is in favour of the workmen: but the 8th of George III is in favour of the masters. When masters combine together in order to reduce the wages of their workmen, they commonly enter into a private bond or agreement not to give more than a certain wage under a certain penalty. Were the workmen to enter into a contrary combination of the same kind, not to accept of a certain wage under a certain penalty, the law would punish them very severely; and if it dealt impartially, it would treat the masters in the same manner. But the 8th of George III enforces by law that very regulation which masters sometimes attempt to establish by such combinations. The complaint of the workmen, that it puts the ablest and most industrious upon the same footing with an ordinary workman, seems perfectly well founded.

In ancient times, too, it was usual to attempt to regulate the profits of merchants and other dealers, by rating the price both of provisions and other goods. The assize of bread is, so far as I know, the only remnant of this ancient usage. Where there is an exclusive corporation, it may perhaps be proper to regulate the price of the first necessary of life. But where there is none, the competition will regulate it much better than any assize. The method of fixing the assize of bread established by the 31st of George II could not be put in practice in Scotland, on account of a defect in the law; its execution depending upon the office of a clerk of the market, which does not exist there. This defect was not remedied till the 3rd of George III. The want of an assize occasioned no sensible inconveniency, and the establishment of one, in the few places where it has yet taken place, has produced no sensible advantage. In the greater part of the towns of Scotland, however, there is an incorporation of bakers who claim exclusive privileges, though they are not very strictly guarded.

The proportion between the different rates both of wages and profit in the different employments of labour and stock, seems not to be much affected, as has already been observed, by the riches or poverty, the advancing, stationary, or declining state of the society. Such revolutions in the public welfare, though they affect the general rates both of wages and profit, must in the end affect them equally in all different employments. The proportion between them, therefore, must remain the same, and cannot well be altered, at least for any considerable time, by any such revolutions.

'The Wealth of Nations', Book 1, Chapter 10, Part 2.

3. FREE TRADE

By restraining, either by high duties or by absolute prohibitions, the importation of such goods from foreign countries as can be produced at home, the monopoly of the home market is more or less secured to the domestic industry employed in producing them. Thus the prohibition of importing either live cattle or salt provisions from foreign countries secures to the graziers of Great Britain the monopoly of the home market for butcher's meat. The high duties upon the importation of corn, which in times of moderate plenty amount to a prohibition, give a like advantage to the growers of that commodity. The prohibition of the importation of foreign woollens is equally favourable to the woollen manufacturers. The silk manufacture, though altogether employed upon foreign materials, has lately obtained the same advantage. The linen manufacture has not yet obtained it, but is making great strides towards it. Many other sorts of manufacturers have, in the same manner, obtained in Great Britain, either altogether or very nearly, a monopoly against their countrymen. The variety of goods of which the importation into Great Britain is prohibited, either absolutely, or under certain circumstances, greatly exceeds what can easily be suspected by those who are not well acquainted with the laws of the customs.

That this monopoly of the home market frequently gives great encouragement to that particular species of industry which enjoys it, and frequently turns towards that employment a greater share of both the labour and stock of the society than would otherwise have gone to it, cannot be doubted. But whether it tends either to increase the general industry of the society, or to give it the most advantageous direction, is not, perhaps, altogether so evident.

The general industry of the society never can exceed what the capital of the society can employ. As the number of workmen that can be kept in employment by any particular person must bear a certain proportion to his capital, so the number of those that can be continually employed by all the members of a great society must bear a certain proportion to the whole capital of that society, and never can exceed that proportion. No regulation of commerce can increase the quantity of industry in any society beyond what its capital can maintain. It can only divert a part of it into a direction into which it might not otherwise have gone; and it is by no means certain that this artificial direction is likely to be more advantageous to the society than that into which it would have gone of its own accord.

Every individual is continually exerting himself to find out the most advantageous employment for whatever capital he can command. It is his own advantage, indeed, and not that of the society, which he has in view. But the study of his own advantage naturally, or rather necessarily, leads him to prefer that employment which is most advantageous to the society.

First, every individual endeavours to employ his capital as near home as he can, and consequently as much as he can in the support of domestic industry; provided always that he can thereby obtain the ordinary, or not a great deal less than the ordinary profits of stock.

Thus, upon equal or nearly equal profits, every wholesale merchant naturally prefers the home trade to the foreign trade of consumption, and the foreign trade of consumption to the carrying trade. In the home trade his capital is never so long out of his sight as it frequently is in the foreign trade of consumption. He can know better the character and situation of the persons whom he trusts, and if he should happen to be deceived, he knows better the laws of the country from which he must seek redress. In the carrying trade, the capital of the merchant is, as it were, divided between two foreign countries, and no part of it is ever necessarily brought home, or placed under his own immediate view and command. The capital which an Amsterdam merchant employs in carrying corn from Konigsberg to Lisbon, and fruit and wine from Lisbon to Konigsberg, must generally be the one half of it at Konigsberg and the other half at Lisbon. No part of it need ever come to Amsterdam. The natural residence of such a merchant should either be at Konigsberg or Lisbon, and it can only be some very particular circumstances which can make him prefer the residence of Amsterdam. The uneasiness, however, which he feels at being separated so far from his capital generally determines him to bring part both of the Konigsberg goods which he destines for the market of Lisbon, and of the Lisbon goods which he destines for that of Konigsberg, to Amsterdam: and though this necessarily subjects him to a double charge of loading and unloading, as well as to the payment of some duties and customs, yet for the sake of having some part of his capital always under his own view and command, he willingly submits to this extraordinary charge; and it is in this manner that every country which has any considerable share of the carrying trade becomes always the emporium, or general market, for the goods of all the different countries whose trade it carries on. The merchant, in order to save a second loading and unloading, endeavours always to sell in the home market as much of the goods of all those different countries as he can, and thus, so far as he can, to convert his carrying trade into a foreign trade of consumption. A merchant, in the same manner, who is engaged in the foreign trade of consumption, when he collects goods for foreign markets, will always be glad, upon equal or nearly equal profits, to sell as great a part of them at home as he can. He saves himself the risk and trouble of exportation, when, so far as he can, he thus converts his foreign trade of consumption into a home trade. Home is in this manner the centre, if I may say so, round which the capitals of the inhabitants of every country are continually circulating, and towards which they are always tending, though by particular causes they may sometimes be driven off and repelled from it towards more distant employments. But a capital employed in the home trade, it has already been shown, necessarily puts into motion a greater quantity of domestic industry, and gives revenue and employment to a greater number of the inhabitants of the country, than an equal capital employed in the foreign trade of consumption: and one employed in the foreign trade of consumption has the same advantage over an equal capital employed in the carrying trade. Upon equal, or only nearly equal profits, therefore, every individual naturally inclines to employ his capital in the manner in which it is likely to afford the greatest support to domestic industry, and to give revenue and employment to the greatest number of people of his own country.

Secondly, every individual who employs his capital in the support of domestic industry, necessarily endeavours so to direct that industry that its produce may be of the greatest possible value.

The produce of industry is what it adds to the subject or materials upon which it is employed. In proportion as the value of this produce is great or small, so will likewise be the profits of the employer. But it is only for the sake of profit that any man employs a capital in the support of industry; and he will always, therefore, endeavour to employ it in the support of that industry of which the produce is likely to be of the greatest value, or to exchange for the greatest quantity either of money or of other goods.

But the annual revenue of every society is always precisely equal to the exchangeable value of the whole annual produce of its industry, or rather is precisely the same thing with that exchangeable value. As every individual, therefore, endeavours as much as he can both to employ his capital in the support of domestic industry, and so to direct that industry that its produce may be of the greatest value; every individual necessarily labours to render the annual revenue of the society as great as he can. He generally, indeed, neither intends to promote the public interest, nor knows how much he is promoting it. By preferring the support of domestic to that of foreign industry, he intends only his own security; and by directing that industry in such a manner as its produce may be of the greatest value, he intends only his own gain, and he is in this, as in many other cases, led by an invisible hand to promote an end which was no part of his intention. Nor is it always the worse for the society that it was no part of it. By pursuing his own interest he frequently promotes that of the society more effectually than when he really intends to promote it. I have never known much good done by those who affected to trade for the public good. It is an affectation, indeed, not very common among merchants, and very few words need be employed in dissuading them from it.

What is the species of domestic industry which his capital can employ, and of which the produce is likely to be of the greatest value, every individual, it is evident, can, in his local situation, judge much better than any statesman or lawgiver can do for him. The statesman who should attempt to direct private people in what manner they ought to employ their capitals would not only load himself with a most unnecessary attention, but assume an authority which could safely be trusted, not only to no single person, but to no council or senate whatever, and which would nowhere be so dangerous as in the hands of a man who had folly and presumption enough to fancy himself fit to exercise it.

To give the monopoly of the home market to the produce of domestic industry, in any particular art or manufacture, is in some measure to direct private people in what manner they ought to employ their capitals, and must, in almost all cases, be either a useless or a hurtful regulation. If the produce of domestic can be brought there as cheap as that of foreign industry, the regulation is evidently useless. If it cannot, it must generally be hurtful. It is the maxim of every prudent master of a family never to attempt to make at home what it will cost him more to make than to buy. The tailor does not attempt to make his own shoes, but buys them of the shoemaker. The shoemaker does not attempt to make his own clothes, but employs a tailor. The farmer attempts to make neither the one nor the other, but employs those different artificers. All of them find it for their interest to employ their whole industry in a way in which they have some advantage over their neighbours, and to purchase with a part of its produce, or what is the same thing, with the price of a part of it, whatever else they have occasion for.

What is prudence in the conduct of every private family can scarce be folly in that of a great kingdom. If a foreign country can supply us with a commodity cheaper than we ourselves can make it, better buy it of them with some part of the produce of our own industry employed in a way in which we have some advantage. The general industry of the country, being always in proportion to the capital which employs it, will not thereby be diminished, no more than that of the above-mentioned artificers; but only left to find out the way in which it can be employed with the greatest advantage. It is certainly not employed to the greatest advantage when it is thus directed towards an object which it can buy cheaper than it can make. The value of its annual produce is certainly more or less diminished when it is thus turned away from producing commodities evidently of more value than the commodity which it is directed to produce. According to the supposition, that commodity could be purchased from foreign countries cheaper than it can be made at home. It could, therefore, have been purchased with a part only of the commodities, or, what is the same thing, with a part only of the price of the commodities, which the industry employed by an equal capital would have produced at home, had it been left to follow its natural course. The industry of the country, therefore, is thus turned away from a more to a less advantageous employment, and the exchangeable value of its annual produce, instead of being increased, according to the intention of the lawgiver, must necessarily be diminished by every such regulation.

By means of such regulations, indeed, a particular manufacture may sometimes be acquired sooner than it could have been otherwise, and after a certain time may be made at home as cheap or cheaper than in the foreign country. But though the industry of the society may be thus carried with advantage into a particular channel sooner than it could have been otherwise, it will by no means follow that the sum total, either of its industry, or of its revenue, can ever be augmented by any such regulation. The industry of the society can augment only in proportion as its capital augments, and its capital can augment only in proportion to what can be gradually saved out of its revenue. But the immediate effect of every such regulation is to diminish its revenue, and what diminishes its revenue is certainly not very likely to augment its capital faster than it would have augmented of its own accord had both capital and industry been left to find out their natural employments.

Though for want of such regulations the society should never acquire the proposed manufacture, it would not, upon that account, necessarily be the poorer in any one period of its duration. In every period of its duration its whole capital and industry might still have been employed, though upon different objects, in the manner that was most advantageous at the time. In every period its revenue might have been the greatest which its capital could afford, and both capital and revenue might have been augmented with the greatest possible rapidity.

The natural advantages which one country has over another in producing particular commodities are sometimes so great that it is acknowledged by all the world to be in vain to struggle with them. By means of glasses, hotbeds, and hot walls, very good grapes can be raised in Scotland, and very good wine too can be made of them at about thirty times the expense for which at least equally good can be brought from foreign countries. Would it be a reasonable law to prohibit the importation of all foreign wines merely to encourage the making of claret and burgundy in Scotland? But if there would be a manifest absurdity in turning towards any employment thirty times more of the capital and industry of the country than would be necessary to purchase from foreign countries an equal quantity of the commodities wanted, there must be an absurdity, though not altogether so glaring, yet exactly of the same kind, in turning towards any such employment a thirtieth, or even a three-hundredth part more of either. Whether the advantages which one country has over another be natural or acquired is in this respect of no consequence. As long as the one country has those advantages, and the other wants them, it will always be more advantageous for the latter rather to buy of the former than to make. It is an acquired advantage only, which one artificer has over his neighbour, who exercises another trade; and yet they both find it more advantageous to buy of one another than to make what does not belong to their particular trades.

Merchants and manufacturers are the people who derive the greatest advantage from this monopoly of the home market. The prohibition of the importation of foreign cattle, and of salt provisions, together with the high duties upon foreign corn, which in times of moderate plenty amount to a prohibition, are not near so advantageous to the graziers and farmers of Great Britain as other regulations of the same kind are to its merchants and manufacturers. Manufactures, those of the finer kind especially, are more easily transported from one country to another than corn or cattle. It is in the fetching and carrying manufactures, accordingly, that foreign trade is chiefly employed. In manufactures, a very small advantage will enable foreigners to undersell our own workmen, even in the home market. It will require a very great one to enable them to do so in the rude produce of the soil. If the free importation of foreign manufactures were permitted, several of the home manufactures would probably suffer, and some of them, perhaps, go to ruin altogether, and a considerable part of the stock and industry at present employed in them would be forced to find out some other employment. But the freest importation of the rude produce of the soil could have no such effect upon the agriculture of the country.

If the importation of foreign cattle, for example, were made ever so free, so few could be imported that the grazing trade of Great Britain could be little affected by it. Live cattle are, perhaps, the only commodity of which the transportation is more expensive by sea than by land. By land they carry themselves to market. By sea, not only the cattle, but their food and their water too, must be carried at no small expense and inconveniency. The short sea between Ireland and Great Britain, indeed, renders the importation of Irish cattle more easy. But though the free importation of them, which was lately permitted only for a limited time, were rendered perpetual, it could have no considerable effect upon the interest of the graziers of Great Britain. Those parts of Great Britain which border upon the Irish Sea are all grazing countries. Irish cattle could never be imported for their use, but must be driven through those very extensive countries, at no small expense and inconveniency, before they could arrive at their proper market. Fat cattle could not be driven so far. Lean cattle, therefore, only could be imported, and such importation could interfere, not with the interest of the feeding or fattening countries, to which, by reducing the price of lean cattle, it would rather be advantageous, but with that of the breeding countries only. The small number of Irish cattle imported since their importation was permitted, together with the good price at which lean cattle still continue to sell, seem to demonstrate that even the breeding countries of Great Britain are never likely to be much affected by the free importation of Irish cattle. The common people of Ireland, indeed, are said to have sometimes opposed with violence the exportation of their cattle. But if the exporters had found any great advantage in continuing the trade, they could easily, when the law was on their side, have conquered this mobbish opposition.

Feeding and fattening countries, besides, must always be highly improved, whereas breeding countries are generally uncultivated. The high price of lean cattle, by augmenting the value of uncultivated land, is like a bounty against improvement. To any country which was highly improved throughout, it would be more advantageous to import its lean cattle than to breed them. The province of Holland, accordingly, is said to follow this maxim at present. The mountains of Scotland, Wales, and Northumberland, indeed, are countries not capable of much improvement, and seem destined by nature to be the breeding countries of Great Britain. The freest importation of foreign cattle could have no other effect than to hinder those breeding countries from taking advantage of the increasing population and improvement of the rest of the kingdom, from raising their price to an exorbitant height, and from laying a real tax upon all the more improved and cultivated parts of the country.

The freest importation of salt provisions, in the same manner, could have as little effect upon the interest of the graziers of Great Britain as that of live cattle. Salt provisions are not only a very bulky commodity, but when compared with fresh meat, they are a commodity both of worse quality, and as they cost more labour and expense, of higher price. They could never, therefore, come into competition with the fresh meat, though they might with the salt provisions of the country. They might be used for victualling ships for distant voyages and such like uses, but could never make any considerable part of the food of the people. The small quantity of salt provisions imported from Ireland since their importation was rendered free is an experimental proof that our graziers have nothing to apprehend from it. It does not appear that the price of butcher's meat has ever been sensibly affected by it.

Even the free importation of foreign corn could very little affect the interest of the farmers of Great Britain. Corn is a much more bulky commodity than butcher's meat. A pound of wheat at a penny is as dear as a pound of butcher's meat at fourpence. The small quantity of foreign corn imported even in times of the greatest scarcity may satisfy our farmers that they can have nothing to fear from the freest importation. The average quantity imported, one year with another, amounts only, according to the very well informed author of the tracts upon the corn trade, to twenty-three thousand seven hundred and twenty-eight quarters of all sorts of grain, and does not exceed the five hundred and seventy-first part of the annual consumption. But as the bounty upon corn occasions a greater exportation in years of plenty, so it must of consequence occasion a greater importation in years of scarcity than in the actual state of tillage would otherwise take place. By means of it the plenty of one year does not compensate the scarcity of another, and as the average quantity exported is necessarily augmented by it, so must likewise, in the actual state of tillage, the average quantity imported. If there were no bounty, as less corn would be exported, so it is probable that, one year with another, less would be imported than at present. The corn-merchants, the fetchers and carriers of corn between Great Britain and foreign countries would have much less employment, and might suffer considerably; but the country gentlemen and farmers could suffer very little. It is in the corn merchants accordingly, rather than in the country gentlemen and farmers, that I have observed the greatest anxiety for the renewal and continuation of the bounty.

Country gentlemen and farmers are, to their great honour, of all people, the least subject to the wretched spirit of monopoly. The undertaker of a great manufactory is sometimes alarmed if another work of the same kind is established within twenty miles of him. The Dutch undertaker of the woollen manufacture at Abbeville stipulated that no work of the same kind should be established within thirty leagues of that city. Farmers and country gentlemen, on the contrary, are generally disposed rather to promote than to obstruct the cultivation and improvement of their neighbours' farms and estates. They have no secrets such as those of the greater part of manufacturers, but are generally rather fond of communicating to their neighbours and of extending as far as possible any new practice which they have found to be advantageous. *Pius Questus*, says old Cato, *stabilissimusque, minimeque invidiosus; minimeque male cogitantes sunt, qui in eo studio occupati sunt.* [It is an honest way of making a living, most steadfast and little envious. They think little evil who are occupied in that field.] Country gentlemen and farmers, dispersed in different parts of the country, cannot so easily combine as merchants and manufacturers, who, being collected into towns, and accustomed to that exclusive corporation spirit which prevails in them, naturally endeavour to obtain against all their countrymen the same exclusive privilege which they generally possess against the inhabitants of their respective towns. They accordingly seem to have been the original inventors of those restraints upon the importation of foreign goods which secure to them the monopoly of the home market. It was probably in imitation of them, and to put themselves upon a level with those who, they found, were disposed to oppress them, that the country gentlemen and farmers of Great Britain in so far forgot the generosity which is natural to their station as to demand the exclusive privilege of supplying their countrymen with corn and butcher's meat. They did not perhaps take time to consider how much less their interest could be affected by the freedom of trade than that of the people whose example they followed.

To prohibit by a perpetual law the importation of foreign corn and cattle is in reality to enact that the population and industry of the country shall at no time exceed what the rude produce of its own soil can maintain.

There seem, however, to be two cases in which it will generally be advantageous to lay some burden upon foreign for the encouragement of domestic industry.

The first is, when some particular sort of industry is necessary for the defence of the country. The defence of Great Britain, for example, depends very much upon the number of its sailors and shipping. The Act of Navigation, therefore, very properly endeavours to give the sailors and shipping of Great Britain the monopoly of the trade of their own country in some cases by absolute prohibitions and in others by heavy burdens upon the shipping of foreign countries. The following are the principal dispositions of this Act.

First, all ships, of which the owners and three-fourths of the mariners are not British subjects, are prohibited, upon pain of forfeiting ship and cargo, from trading to the British settlements and plantations, or from being employed in the coasting trade of Great Britain.

Secondly, a great variety of the most bulky articles of importation can be brought into Great Britain only, either in such ships as are above described, or in ships of the country where those goods are purchased, and of which the owners, masters, and three-fourths of the mariners are of that particular country; and when imported even in ships of this latter kind, they are subject to double aliens' duty. If imported in ships of any other country, the penalty is forfeiture of ship and goods. When this act was made, the Dutch were, what they still are, the great carriers of Europe, and by this regulation they were entirely excluded from being the carriers to Great Britain, or from importing to us the goods of any other European country.

Thirdly, a great variety of the most bulky articles of importation are prohibited from being imported, even in British ships, from any country but that in which they are produced, under pains of forfeiting ship and cargo. This regulation, too, was probably intended against the Dutch. Holland was then, as now, the great emporium for all European goods, and by this regulation British ships were hindered from loading in Holland the goods of any other European country.

Fourthly, salt fish of all kinds, whale-fins, whale-bone, oil, and blubber, not caught by and cured on board British vessels, when imported into Great Britain, are subjected to double aliens' duty. The Dutch, as they are they the principal, were then the only fishers in Europe that attempted to supply foreign nations with fish. By this regulation, a very heavy burden was laid upon their supplying Great Britain.

When the Act of Navigation was made, though England and Holland were not actually at war, the most violent animosity subsisted between the two nations. It had begun during the government of the Long Parliament, which first framed this act, and it broke out soon after in the Dutch wars during that of the Protector and of Charles the Second. It is not impossible, therefore, that some of the regulations of this famous act may have proceeded from national animosity. They are as wise, however, as if they had all been dictated by the most deliberate wisdom. National animosity at that particular time aimed at the very same object which the most deliberate wisdom would have recommended, the diminution of the naval power of Holland, the only naval power which could endanger the security of England.

The Act of Navigation is not favourable to foreign commerce, or to the growth of that opulence which can arise from it. The interest of a nation in its commercial relations to foreign nations is, like that of a merchant with regard to the different people with whom he deals, to buy as cheap and to sell as dear as possible. But it will be most likely to buy cheap, when by the most perfect freedom of trade it encourages all nations to bring to it the goods which it has occasion to purchase; and, for the same reason, it will be most likely to sell dear, when its markets are thus filled with the greatest number of buyers. The Act of Navigation, it is true, lays no burden upon foreign ships that come to export the produce of British industry. Even the ancient aliens' duty, which used to be paid upon all goods exported as well as imported, has, by several subsequent acts, been taken off from the greater part of the articles of exportation. But if foreigners, either by prohibitions or high duties, are hindered from coming to sell, they cannot always afford to come to buy; because coming without a cargo, they must lose the freight from their own country to Great Britain. By diminishing the number of sellers, therefore, we necessarily diminish that of buyers, and are thus likely not only to buy foreign goods dearer, but to sell our own cheaper, than if there was a more perfect freedom of trade. As defence, however it is of much more importance than opulence, the Act of Navigation is, perhaps, the wisest of all the commercial regulations of England.

The second case, in which it will generally be advantageous to lay some burden upon foreign for the encouragement of domestic industry is, when some tax is imposed at home upon the produce of the latter. In this case, it seems reasonable that an equal tax should be imposed upon the like produce of the former. This would not give the monopoly of the home market to domestic industry, nor turn towards a particular employment a greater share of the stock and labour of the country than what would naturally go to it. It would only hinder any part of what would naturally go to it from being turned away by the tax into a less natural direction, and would leave the competition between foreign and domestic industry, after the tax, as nearly as possible upon the same footing as before it. In Great Britain, when any such tax is laid upon the produce of domestic industry, it is usual at the same time, in order to stop the clamorous complaints of our merchants and manufacturers that they will be undersold at home, to lay a much heavier duty upon the importation of all foreign goods of the same kind.

This second limitation of the freedom of trade according to some people should, upon some occasions, be extended much farther than to the precise foreign commodities which could come into competition with those which had been taxed at home. When the necessaries of life have been taxed any country, it becomes proper, they pretend, to tax not only the like necessaries of life imported from other countries, but all sorts of foreign goods which can come into competition with anything that is the produce of domestic industry. Subsistence, they say, becomes necessarily dearer in consequence of such taxes; and the price of labour must always rise with the price of the labourers' subsistence. Every commodity, therefore, which is the produce of domestic industry, though not immediately taxed itself, becomes dearer in consequence of such taxes, because the labour which produces it becomes so. Such taxes, therefore, are really equivalent, they say, to a tax upon every particular commodity produced at home. In order to put domestic upon the same footing with foreign industry, therefore, it becomes necessary, they think, to lay some duty upon every foreign commodity equal to this enhancement of the price of the home commodities with which it can come into competition.

Whether taxes upon the necessaries of life, such as those in Great Britain upon soap, salt, leather, candles, etc., necessarily raise the price of labour, and consequently that of all other commodities, I shall consider hereafter when I come to treat of taxes. Supposing, however, in the meantime, that they have this effect, and they have it undoubtedly, this general enhancement of the price of all commodities, in consequence of that of labour, is a case which differs in the two following respects from that of a particular commodity of which the price was enhanced by a particular tax immediately imposed upon it.

First, it might always be known with great exactness how far the price of such a commodity could be enhanced by such a tax: but how far the general enhancement of the price of labour might affect that of every different commodity about which labour was employed could never be known with any tolerable exactness. It would be impossible, therefore, to proportion with any tolerable exactness the tax upon every foreign to this enhancement of the price of every home commodity.

Secondly, taxes upon the necessaries of life have nearly the same effect upon the circumstances of the people as a poor soil and a bad climate. Provisions are thereby rendered dearer in the same manner as if it required extraordinary labour and expense to raise them. As in the natural scarcity arising from soil and climate it would be absurd to direct the people in what manner they ought to employ their capitals and industry, so is it likewise in the artificial scarcity arising from such taxes. To be left to accommodate, as well as they could, their industry to their situation, and to find out those employments in which, notwithstanding their unfavourable circumstances, they might have some advantage either in the home or in the foreign market, is what in both cases would evidently be most for their advantage. To lay a new tax upon them, because they are already overburdened with taxes, and because they already pay too dear for the necessaries of life, to make them likewise pay too dear for the greater part of other commodities, is certainly a most absurd way of making amends.

Such taxes, when they have grown up to a certain height, are a curse equal to the barrenness of the earth and the inclemency of the heavens; and yet it is in the richest and most industrious countries that they have been most generally imposed. No other countries could support so great a disorder. As the strongest bodies only can live and enjoy health under an unwholesome regimen, so the nations only that in every sort of industry have the greatest natural and acquired advantages can subsist and prosper under such taxes. Holland is the country in Europe in which they abound most, and which from peculiar circumstances continues to prosper, not by means of them, as has been most absurdly supposed, but in spite of them.

As there are two cases in which it will generally be advantageous to lay some burden upon foreign for the encouragement of domestic industry, so there are two others in which it may sometimes be a matter of deliberation; in the one, how far it is proper to continue the free importation of certain foreign goods; and in the other, how far, or in what manner, it may be proper to restore that free importation after it has been for some time interrupted.

The case in which it may sometimes be a matter of deliberation how far it is proper to continue the free importation of certain foreign goods is, when some foreign nation restrains by high duties or prohibitions the importation of some of our manufactures into their country. Revenge in this case naturally dictates retaliation, and that we should impose the like duties and prohibitions upon the importation of some or all of their manufactures into ours. Nations, accordingly, seldom fail to retaliate in this manner. The French have been particularly forward to favour their own manufactures by restraining the importation of such foreign goods as could come into competition with them. In this consisted a great part of the policy of Mr. Colbert, who, notwithstanding his great abilities, seems in this case to have been imposed upon by the sophistry of merchants and manufacturers, who are always demanding a monopoly against their countrymen. It is at present the opinion of the most intelligent men in France that his operations of this kind have not been beneficial to his country. That minister, by the tariff of 1667, imposed very high duties upon a great number of foreign manufactures. Upon his refusing to moderate them in favour of the Dutch, they in 1671 prohibited the importation of the wines, brandies, and manufactures of France. The war of 1672 seems to have been in part occasioned by this commercial dispute. The peace of Nimeguen put an end to it in 1678 by moderating some of those duties in favour of the Dutch, who in consequence took off their prohibition. It was about the same time that the French and English began mutually to oppress each other's industry by the like duties and prohibitions, of which the French, however, seem to have set the first example. The spirit of hostility which has subsisted between the two nations ever since has hitherto hindered them from being moderated on either side. In 1697 the English prohibited the importation of bonelace, the manufacture of Flanders. The government of that country, at that time under the dominion of Spain, prohibited in return the importation of English woollens. In 1700, the prohibition of importing bonelace into England was taken off upon condition that the importance of English woollens into Flanders should be put on the same footing as before.

There may be good policy in retaliations of this kind, when there is a probability that they will procure the repeal of the high duties or prohibitions complained of. The recovery of a great foreign market will generally more than compensate the transitory inconveniency of paying dearer during a short time for some sorts of goods. To judge whether such retaliations are likely to produce such an effect does not, perhaps, belong so much to the science of a legislator, whose deliberations ought to be governed by general principles which are always the same, as to the skill of that insidious and crafty animal, vulgarly called a statesman or politician, whose councils are directed by the momentary fluctuations of affairs. When there is no probability that any such repeal can be procured, it seems a bad method of compensating the injury done to certain classes of our people to do another injury ourselves, not only to those classes, but to almost all the other classes of them. When our neighbours prohibit some manufacture of ours, we generally prohibit, not only the same, for that alone would seldom affect them considerably, but some other manufacture of theirs. This may no doubt give encouragement to some particular class of workmen among ourselves, and by excluding some of their rivals, may enable them to raise their price in the home market. Those workmen, however, who suffered by our neighbours' prohibition will not be benefited by ours. On the contrary, they and almost all the other classes of our citizens will thereby be obliged to pay dearer than before for certain goods. Every such law, therefore, imposes a real tax upon the whole country, not in favour of that particular class of workmen who were injured by our neighbours' prohibition, but of some other class.

The case in which it may sometimes be a matter of deliberation, how far, or in what manner, it is proper to restore the free importation of foreign goods, after it has been for some time interrupted, is, when particular manufactures, by means of high duties or prohibitions upon all foreign goods which can come into competition with them, have been so far extended as to employ a great multitude of hands. Humanity may in this case require that the freedom of trade should be restored only by slow gradations, and with a good deal of reserve and circumspection. Were those high duties and prohibitions taken away all at once, cheaper foreign goods of the same kind might be poured so fast into the home market as to deprive all at once many thousands of our people of their ordinary employment and means of subsistence. The disorder which this would occasion might no doubt be very considerable. It would in all probability, however, be much less than is commonly imagined, for the two following reasons:-

First, all those manufactures, of which any part is commonly exported to other European countries without a bounty, could be very little affected by the freest importation of foreign goods. Such manufactures must be sold as cheap abroad as any other foreign goods of the same quality and kind, and consequently must be sold cheaper at home. They would still, therefore, keep possession of the home market, and though a capricious man of fashion might sometimes prefer foreign wares, merely because they were foreign, to cheaper and better goods of the same kind that were made at home, this folly could, from the nature of things, extend to so few that it could make no sensible impression upon the general employment of the people. But a great part of all the different branches of our woollen manufacture, of our tanned leather, and of our hardware, are annually exported to other European countries without any bounty, and these are the manufactures which employ the greatest number of hands. The silk, perhaps, is the manufacture which would suffer the most by this freedom of trade, and after it the linen, though the latter much less than the former.

Secondly, though a great number of people should, by thus restoring the freedom of trade, be thrown all at once out of their ordinary employment and common method of subsistence, it would by no means follow that they would thereby be deprived either of employment or subsistence. By the reduction of the army and navy at the end of the late war, more than a hundred thousand soldiers and seamen, a number equal to what is employed in the greatest manufactures, were all at once thrown out of their ordinary employment; but, though they no doubt suffered some inconveniency, they were not thereby deprived of all employment and subsistence. The greater part of the seamen, it is probable, gradually betook themselves to the merchant-service as they could find occasion, and in the meantime both they and the soldiers were absorbed in the great mass of the people, and employed in a great variety of occupations. Not only no great convulsion, but no sensible disorder arose from so great a change in the situation of more than a hundred thousand men, all accustomed to the use of arms, and many of them to rapine and plunder. The number of vagrants was scarce anywhere sensibly increased by it, even the wages of labour were not reduced by it in any occupation, so far as I have been able to learn, except in that of seamen in the merchant service. But if we compare together the habits of a soldier and of any sort of manufacturer, we shall find that those of the latter do not tend so much to disqualify him from being employed in a new trade, as those of the former from being employed in any. The manufacturer has always been accustomed to look for his subsistence from his labour only: the soldier to expect it from his pay. Application and industry have been familiar to the one; idleness and dissipation to the other. But it is surely much easier to change the direction of industry from one sort of labour to another than to turn idleness and dissipation to any. To the greater part of manufactures besides, it has already been observed, there are other collateral manufactures of so similar a nature that a workman can easily transfer his industry from one of them to another. The greater part of such workmen too are occasionally employed in country labour. The stock which employed them in a particular manufacture before will still remain in the country to employ an equal number of people in some other way. The capital of the country remaining the same, the demand for labour will likewise be the same, or very nearly the same, though it may be exerted in different places and for different occupations. Soldiers and seamen, indeed, when discharged from the king's service, are at liberty to exercise any trade, within any town or place of Great Britain or Ireland. Let the same natural liberty of exercising what species of industry they please, be restored to all his Majesty's subjects, in the same manner as to soldiers and seamen; that is, break down the exclusive privileges of corporations, and repeal the Statute of Apprenticeship, both which are real encroachments upon natural liberty, and add to these the repeal of the Law of Settlements, so that a poor workman, when thrown out of employment either in one trade or in one place, may seek for it in another trade or in another place without the fear either of a prosecution or of a removal, and neither the public nor the individuals will suffer much more from the occasional disbanding some particular classes of manufacturers than from that of soldiers. Our manufacturers have no doubt great merit with their country, but they cannot have more than those who defend it with their blood, nor deserve to be treated with more delicacy.

To expect, indeed, that the freedom of trade should ever be entirely restored in Great Britain is as absurd as to expect that an Oceana or Utopia should ever be established in it. Not only the prejudices of the public, but what is much more unconquerable, the private interests of many individuals, irresistibly oppose it. Were the officers of the army to oppose with the same zeal and unanimity any reduction in the numbers of forces with which master manufacturers set themselves against every law that is likely to increase the number of their rivals in the home market; were the former to animate their soldiers in the same manner as the latter enflame their workmen to attack with violence and outrage the proposers of any such regulation, to attempt to reduce the army would be as dangerous as it has now become to attempt to diminish in any respect the monopoly which our manufacturers have obtained against us. This monopoly has so much increased the number of some particular tribes of them that, like an overgrown standing army, they have become formidable to the government, and upon many occasions intimidate the legislature. The Member of Parliament who supports every proposal for strengthening this monopoly is sure to acquire not only the reputation of understanding trade, but great popularity and influence with an order of men whose numbers and wealth render them of great importance. If he opposes them, on the contrary, and still more if he has authority enough to be able to thwart them, neither the most acknowledged probity, nor the highest rank, nor the greatest public services can protect him from the most infamous abuse and detraction, from personal insults, nor sometimes from real danger, arising from the insolent outrage of furious and disappointed monopolists.

The undertaker of a great manufacture, who, by the home markets being suddenly laid open to the competition of foreigners, should be obliged to abandon his trade, would no doubt suffer very considerably. That part of his capital which had usually been employed in purchasing materials and in paying his workmen might, without much difficulty, perhaps, find another employment. But that part of it which was fixed in workhouses, and in the instruments of trade, could scarce be disposed of without considerable loss. The equitable regard, therefore, to his interest requires that changes of this kind should never be introduced suddenly, but slowly, gradually, and after a very long warning. The legislature, were it possible that its deliberations could be always directed, not by the clamorous importunity of partial interests, but by an extensive view of the general good, ought upon this very account, perhaps, to be particularly careful neither to establish any new monopolies of this kind, nor to extend further those which are already established. Every such regulation introduces some degree of real disorder into the constitution of the state, which it will be difficult afterwards to cure without occasioning another disorder.

How far it may be proper to impose taxes upon the importation of foreign goods, in order not to prevent their importation but to raise a revenue for government, I shall consider hereafter when I

come to treat of taxes. Taxes imposed with a view to prevent, or even to diminish importation, are evidently as destructive of the revenue of the customs as of the freedom of trade.
'The Wealth of Nations,' Book 4, Chapter 2.

4. PRODUCTIVE AND UNPRODUCTIVE LABOUR

There is one sort of labour which adds to the value of the subject upon which it is bestowed: there is another which has no such effect. The former, as it produces a value, may be called productive; the latter, unproductive labour. Thus the labour of a manufacturer adds, generally, to the value of the materials which he works upon, that of his own maintenance, and of his master's profit. The labour of a menial servant, on the contrary, adds to the value of nothing. Though the manufacturer has his wages advanced to him by his master, he, in reality, costs him no expense, the value of those wages being generally restored, together with a profit, in the improved value of the subject upon which his labour is bestowed. But the maintenance of a menial servant never is restored. A man grows rich by employing a multitude of manufacturers: he grows poor by maintaining a multitude of menial servants. The labour of the latter, however, has its value, and deserves its reward as well as that of the former. But the labour of the manufacturer fixes and realizes itself in some particular subject or vendible commodity, which lasts for some time at least after that labour is past. It is, as it were, a certain quantity of labour stocked and stored up to be employed, if necessary, upon some other occasion. That subject, or what is the same thing, the price of that subject, can afterwards, if necessary, put into motion a quantity of labour equal to that which had originally produced it. The labour of the menial servant, on the contrary, does not fix or realize itself in any particular subject or vendible commodity. His services generally perish in the very instant of their performance, and seldom leave any trace or value behind them for which an equal quantity of service could afterwards be procured.

The labour of some of the most respectable orders in the society is, like that of menial servants, unproductive of any value, and does not fix or realize itself in any permanent subject; or vendible commodity, which endures after that labour is past, and for which an equal quantity of labour could afterwards be procured. The sovereign, for example, with all the officers both of justice and war who serve under him, the whole army and navy, are unproductive labourers. They are the servants of the public, and are maintained by a part of the annual produce of the industry of other people. Their service, how honourable, how useful, or how necessary soever, produces nothing for which an equal quantity of service can afterwards be procured. The protection, security, and defence of the commonwealth, the effect of their labour this year will not purchase its protection, security, and defence for the year to come. In the same class must be ranked, some both of the gravest and most important, and some of the most frivolous professions: churchmen, lawyers, physicians, men of letters of all kinds; players, buffoons, musicians, opera-singers, opera-dancers, etc. The labour of the meanest of these has a certain value, regulated by the very same principles which regulate that of every other sort of labour; and that of the noblest and most useful produces nothing which could afterwards purchase or procure an equal quantity of labour. Like the declamation of the actor, the harangue of the orator, or the tune of the musician, the work of all of them perishes in the very instant of its production.

Both productive and unproductive labourers, and those who do not labour at all, are all equally maintained by the annual produce of the land and labour of the country. This produce, how great soever, can never be infinite, but must have certain limits. According, therefore, as a smaller or greater proportion of it is in any one year employed in maintaining unproductive hands, the more in the one case and the less in the other will remain for the productive, and the next year's produce will be greater or smaller accordingly; the whole annual produce, if we except the spontaneous productions of the earth, being the effect of productive labour.

Though the whole annual produce of the land and labour of every country is, no doubt, ultimately destined for supplying the consumption of its inhabitants, and for procuring a revenue to them, yet when it first comes either from the ground, or from the hands of the productive labourers, it naturally divides itself into two parts. One of them, and frequently the largest, is, in the first place, destined for replacing a capital, or for renewing the provisions, materials, and finished work, which had been withdrawn from a capital; the other for constituting a revenue either to the owner of this capital, as the profit of his stock, or to some other person, as the rent of his land. Thus, of the produce of land, one part replaces the capital of the farmer; the other pays his profit and the rent of the landlord; and thus constitutes a revenue both to the owner of this capital, as the profits of his stock; and to some other person, as the rent of his land. Of the produce of a great manufactory, in the same manner, one part, and that always the largest, replaces the capital of the undertaker of the work; the other pays his profit, and thus constitutes a revenue to the owner of this capital.

That part of the annual produce of the land and labour of any country which replaces a capital never is immediately employed to maintain any but productive hands. It pays the wages of productive labour only. That which is immediately destined for constituting a revenue, either as profit or as rent, may maintain indifferently either productive or unproductive hands.

Whatever part of his stock a man employs as a capital, he always expects is to be replaced to him with a profit. He employs it, therefore, in maintaining productive hands only; and after having served in the function of a capital to him, it constitutes a revenue to them. Whenever he employs any part of it in maintaining unproductive hands of any kind, that part is, from that moment, withdrawn from his capital, and placed in his stock reserved for immediate consumption.

Unproductive labourers, and those who do not labour at all, are all maintained by revenue; either, first, by that part of the annual produce which is originally destined for constituting a revenue to some particular persons, either as the rent of land or as the profits of stock; or, secondly, by that part which, though originally destined for replacing a capital and for maintaining productive labourers only, yet when it comes into their hands whatever part of it is over and above their necessary subsistence may be employed in maintaining indifferently either productive or unproductive hands. Thus, not only the great landlord or the rich merchant, but even the common workman, if his wages are considerable, may maintain a menial servant; or he may sometimes go to a play or a puppetshow, and so contribute his share towards maintaining one set of unproductive labourers; or he may pay some taxes, and thus help to maintain another set, more honourable and useful indeed, but equally unproductive. No part of the annual produce, however, which had been originally destined to replace a capital, is ever directed towards maintaining unproductive hands till after it has put into motion its full complement of productive labour, or all that it could put into motion in the way in which it was employed. The workman must have earned his wages by work done before he can employ any part of them in this manner. That part, too, is generally but a small one. It is his spare revenue only, of which productive labourers have seldom a great deal. They generally have some, however; and in the payment of taxes the greatness of their number may compensate, in some measure, the smallness of their contribution. The rent of land and the profits of stock are everywhere, therefore, the principal sources from which unproductive hands derive their subsistence. These are the two sorts of revenue of which the owners have generally most to spare. They might both maintain indifferently either productive or unproductive hands. They seem, however, to have some predilection for the latter. The expense of a great lord feeds generally more idle than industrious people. The rich merchant, though with his capital he maintains industrious people only, yet by his expense, that is, by the employment of his revenue, he feeds commonly the very same sort as the great lord.

The proportion, therefore, between the productive and unproductive hands, depends very much in every country upon the proportion between that part of the annual produce, which, as soon as it comes either from the ground or from the hands of the productive labourers, is destined for replacing a capital, and that which is destined for constituting a revenue, either as rent or as profit. This proportion is very different in rich from what it is in poor countries.

Thus, at present, in the opulent countries of Europe, a very large, frequently the largest portion of the produce of the land is destined for replacing the capital of the rich and independent farmer; the other for paying his profits and the rent of the landlord. But anciently, during the prevalency of the feudal government, a very small portion of the produce was sufficient to replace the capital employed in cultivation. It consisted commonly in a few wretched cattle, maintained altogether by the spontaneous produce of uncultivated land, and which might, therefore, be considered as a part of that spontaneous produce. It generally, too, belonged to the landlord, and was by him advanced to the occupiers of the land. All the rest of the produce properly belonged to him too, either as rent for his land, or as profit upon this paltry capital. The occupiers of land were generally bondmen, whose persons and effects were equally his property. Those who were not bondmen were tenants at will, and though the rent which they paid was often nominally little more than a quit-rent, it really amounted to the whole produce of the land. Their lord could at all times command their labour in peace and their service in war. Though they lived at a distance from his house, they were equally dependent upon him as his retainers who lived in it. But the whole produce of the land undoubtedly belongs to him who can dispose of the labour and service of all those whom it maintains. In the present state of Europe, the share of the landlord seldom exceeds a third, sometimes not a fourth part of the whole produce of the land. The rent of land, however, in all the improved parts of the country, has been tripled and quadrupled since those ancient times; and this third or fourth part of the annual produce is, it seems, three or four times greater than the whole had been before. In the progress of improvement, rent, though it increases in proportion to the extent, diminishes in proportion to the produce of the land.

In the opulent countries of Europe, great capitals are at present employed in trade and manufactures. In the ancient state, the little trade that was stirring, and the few homely and coarse manufactures that were carried on, required but very small capitals. These, however, must have yielded very large profits. The rate of interest was nowhere less than ten per cent, and their profits must have been sufficient to afford this great interest. At present the rate of interest, in the improved parts of Europe, is nowhere higher than six per cent, and in some of the most improved it is so low as four, three, and two per cent. Though that part of the revenue of the inhabitants which is derived from the profits of stock is always much greater in rich than in poor countries, it is because the stock is much greater: in proportion to the stock the profits are generally much less.

That part of the annual produce, therefore, which, as soon as it comes either from the ground or from the hands of the productive labourers, is destined for replacing a capital, is not only much greater in rich than in poor countries, but bears a much greater proportion to that which is immediately destined for constituting a revenue either as rent or as profit. The funds destined for the maintenance of productive labour are not only much greater in the former than in the latter, but bear a much greater proportion to those which, though they may be employed to maintain either productive or unproductive hands, have generally a predilection for the latter.

The proportion between those different funds necessarily determines in every country the general character of the inhabitants as to industry or idleness. We are more industrious than our forefathers; because in the present times the funds destined for the maintenance of industry are much greater in proportion to those which are likely to be employed in the maintenance of idleness than they were two or three centuries ago. Our ancestors were idle for want of a sufficient encouragement to industry. It is better, says the proverb, to play for nothing than to work for nothing. In mercantile and manufacturing towns, where the inferior ranks of people are chiefly maintained by the employment of capital, they are in general industrious, sober, and thriving; as in many English, and in most Dutch towns. In those towns which are principally supported by the constant or occasional residence of a court, and in which the inferior ranks of people are chiefly maintained by the spending of revenue, they are in general idle, dissolute, and poor; as at Rome, Versailles, Compiegne, and Fontainebleu. If you except Rouen and Bordeaux, there is little trade or industry in any of the parliament towns of France; and the inferior ranks of people, being chiefly maintained by the expense of the members of the courts of justice, and of those who come to plead before them, are in general idle and poor. The great trade of Rouen and Bordeaux seems to be altogether the effect of their situation. Rouen is necessarily the entrepot of almost all the goods which are brought either from foreign countries, or from the maritime provinces of France, for the consumption of the great city of Paris. Bordeaux is in the same manner the entrepot of the wines which grow upon the banks of the Garonne, and of the rivers which run into it, one of the richest wine countries in the world, and which seems to produce the wine fittest for exportation, or best suited to the taste of foreign nations. Such advantageous situations necessarily attract a great capital by the great employment which they afford it; and the employment of this capital is the cause of the industry of those two cities. In the other parliament towns of France, very little more capital seems to be employed than what is necessary for supplying their own consumption;

that is, little more than the smallest capital which can be employed in them. The same thing may be said of Paris, Madrid, and Vienna. Of those three cities, Paris is by far the most industrious; but Paris itself is the principal market of all the manufactures established at Paris, and its own consumption is the principal object of all the trade which it carries on. London, Lisbon, and Copenhagen, are, perhaps, the only three cities in Europe which are both the constant residence of a court, and can at the same time be considered as trading cities, or as cities which trade not only for their own consumption, but for that of other cities and countries. The situation of all the three is extremely advantageous, and naturally fits them to be the entrepots of a great part of the goods destined for the consumption of distant places. In a city where a great revenue is spent, to employ with advantage a capital for any other purpose than for supplying the consumption of that city is probably more difficult than in one in which the inferior ranks of people have no other maintenance but what they derive from the employment of such a capital. The idleness of the greater part of the people who are maintained by the expense of revenue corrupts, it is probable, the industry of those who ought to be maintained by the employment of capital, and renders it less advantageous to employ a capital there than in other places. There was little trade or industry in Edinburgh before the union. When the Scotch Parliament was no longer to be assembled in it, when it ceased to be the necessary residence of the principal nobility and gentry of Scotland, it became a city of some trade and industry. It still continues, however, to be the residence of the principal courts of justice in Scotland, of the Boards of Customs and Excise, etc. A considerable revenue, therefore, still continues to be spent in it. In trade and industry it is much inferior to Glasgow, of which the inhabitants are chiefly maintained by the employment of capital. The inhabitants of a large village, it has sometimes been observed, after having made considerable progress in manufactures, have become idle and poor in consequence of a great lord having taken up his residence in their neighbourhood.

The proportion between capital and revenue, therefore, seems everywhere to regulate the proportion between industry and idleness. Wherever capital predominates, industry prevails: wherever revenue, idleness. Every increase or diminution of capital, therefore, naturally tends to increase or diminish the real quantity of industry, the number of productive hands, and consequently the exchangeable value of the annual produce of the land and labour of the country, the real wealth and revenue of all its inhabitants.

Capitals are increased by parsimony, and diminished by prodigality and misconduct.

Whatever a person saves from his revenue he adds to his capital, and either employs it himself in maintaining an additional number of productive hands, or enables some other person to do so, by lending it to him for an interest, that is, for a share of the profits. As the capital of an individual can be increased only by what he saves from his annual revenue or his annual gains, so the capital of a society, which is the same with that of all the individuals who compose it, can be increased only in the same manner.

Parsimony, and not industry, is the immediate cause of the increase of capital. Industry, indeed, provides the subject which parsimony accumulates. But whatever industry might acquire, if parsimony did not save and store up, the capital would never be the greater.

Parsimony, by increasing the fund which is destined for the maintenance of productive hands, tends to increase the number of those hands whose labour adds to the value of the subject upon which it is bestowed. It tends, therefore, to increase the exchangeable value of the annual produce of the land and labour of the country. It puts into motion an additional quantity of industry, which gives an additional value to the annual produce.

What is annually saved is as regularly consumed as what is annually spent, and nearly in the same time too; but it is consumed by a different set of people. That portion of his revenue which a rich man annually spends is in most cases consumed by idle guests and menial servants, who leave nothing behind them in return for their consumption. That portion which he annually saves, as for the sake of the profit it is immediately employed as a capital, is consumed in the same manner, and nearly in the same time too, but by a different set of people, by labourers, manufacturers, and artificers, who reproduce with a profit the value of their annual consumption. His revenue, we shall suppose, is paid him in money. Had he spent the whole, the food, clothing, and lodging, which the whole could have purchased, would have been distributed among the former set of people. By saving a part of it, as that part is for the sake of the profit immediately employed as a capital either by himself or by some other person, the food, clothing, and lodging, which may be purchased with it, are necessarily reserved for the latter. The consumption is the same, but the consumers are different.

By what a frugal man annually saves, he not only affords maintenance to an additional number of productive hands, for that or the ensuing year, but, like the founder of a public workhouse, he establishes as it were a perpetual fund for the maintenance of an equal number in all times to come. The perpetual allotment and destination of this fund, indeed, is not always guarded by any positive law, by any trust-right or deed of mortmain. It is always guarded, however, by a very powerful principle, the plain and evident interest of every individual to whom any share of it shall ever belong. No part of it can ever afterwards be employed to maintain any but productive hands without an evident loss to the person who thus perverts it from its proper destination.

The prodigal perverts it in this manner. By not confining his expense within his income, he encroaches upon his capital. Like him who perverts the revenues of some pious foundation to profane purposes, he pays the wages of idleness with those funds which the frugality of his forefathers had, as it were, consecrated to the maintenance of industry. By diminishing the funds destined for the employment of productive labour, he necessarily diminishes, so far as it depends upon him, the quantity of that labour which adds a value to the subject upon which it is bestowed, and, consequently, the value of the annual produce of the land and labour of the whole country, the real wealth and revenue of its inhabitants. If the prodigality of some was not compensated by the frugality of others, the conduct of every prodigal, by feeding the idle with the bread of the industrious, tends not only to beggar himself, but to impoverish his country.

Though the expense of the prodigal should be altogether in home-made, and no part of it in foreign commodities, its effect upon the productive funds of the society would still be the same. Every year there would still be a certain quantity of food and clothing, which ought to have maintained productive, employed in maintaining unproductive hands. Every year, therefore, there would still be some diminution in what would otherwise have been the value of the annual produce of the land and labour of the country.

This expense, it may be said indeed, not being in foreign goods, and not occasioning any exportation of gold and silver, the same quantity of money would remain in the country as before. But if the quantity of food and clothing, which were thus consumed by unproductive, had been distributed among productive hands, they would have reproduced, together with a profit, the full value of their consumption. The same quantity of money would in this case equally have remained in the country, and there would besides have been a reproduction of an equal value of consumable goods. There would have been two values instead of one.

The same quantity of money, besides, cannot long remain in any country in which the value of the annual produce diminishes. The sole use of money is to circulate consumable goods. By means of it, provisions, materials, and finished work, are bought and sold, and distributed to their proper consumers. The quantity of money, therefore, which can be annually employed in any country must be determined by the value of the consumable goods annually circulated within it. These must consist either in the immediate produce of the land and labour of the country itself, or in something which had been, purchased with some part of that produce. Their value, therefore, must diminish as the value of that produce diminishes, and along with it the quantity of money which can be employed in circulating them. But the money which by this annual diminution of produce is annually thrown out of domestic circulation will not be allowed to lie idle. The interest of whoever possesses it requires that it should be employed. But having no employment at home, it will, in spite of all laws and prohibitions, be sent abroad, and employed in purchasing consumable goods which may be of some use at home. Its annual exportation will in this manner continue for some time to add something to the annual consumption of the country beyond the value of its own annual produce. What in the days of its prosperity had been saved from that annual produce, and employed in purchasing gold and silver, will contribute for some little time to support its consumption in adversity.

The exportation of gold and silver is, in this case, not the cause, but the effect of its declension, and may even, for some little time, alleviate the misery of that declension.

The quantity of money, on the contrary, must in every country naturally increase as the value of the annual produce increases. The value of the consumable goods annually circulated within the society being greater will require a greater quantity of money to circulate them. A part of the increased produce, therefore, will naturally be employed in purchasing, wherever it is to be had, the additional quantity of gold and silver necessary for circulating the rest. The increase of those metals will in this case be the effect, not the cause, of the public prosperity. Gold and silver are purchased everywhere in the same manner. The food, clothing, and lodging, the revenue and maintenance of all those whose labour or stock is employed in bringing them from the mine to the market, is the price paid for them in Peru as well as in England. The country which has this price to pay will never be long without the quantity of those metals which it has occasion for; and no country will ever long retain a quantity which it has no occasion for.

Whatever, therefore, we may imagine the real wealth and revenue of a country to consist in, whether in the value of the annual produce of its land and labour, as plain reason seems to dictate; or in the quantity of the precious metals which circulate within it, as vulgar prejudices suppose; in either view of the matter, every prodigal appears to be a public enemy, and every frugal man a public benefactor.

The effects of misconduct are often the same as those of prodigality. Every injudicious and unsuccessful project in agriculture, mines, fisheries, trade, or manufactures, tends in the same manner to diminish the funds destined for the maintenance of productive labour. In every such project, though the capital is consumed by productive hands only, yet, as by the injudicious manner in which they are employed they do not reproduce the full value of their consumption, there must always be some diminution in what would otherwise have been the productive funds of the society.

It can seldom happen, indeed, that the circumstances of a great nation can be much affected either by the prodigality or misconduct of individuals; the profusion or imprudence of some being always more than compensated by the frugality and good conduct of others.

With regard to profusion, the principle which prompts to expense is the passion for present enjoyment; which, though sometimes violent and very difficult to be restrained, is in general only momentary and occasional. But the principle which prompts to save is the desire of bettering our condition, a desire which, though generally calm and dispassionate, comes with us from the womb, and never leaves us till we go into the grave. In the whole interval which separates those two moments, there is scarce perhaps a single instant in which any man is so perfectly and completely satisfied with his situation as to be without any wish of alteration or improvement of any kind. An augmentation of fortune is the means by which the greater part of men propose and wish to better their condition. It is the means the most vulgar and the most obvious; and the most likely way of augmenting their fortune is to save and accumulate some part of what they acquire, either regularly and annually, or upon some extraordinary occasions. Though the principle of expense, therefore, prevails in almost all men upon some occasions, and in some men upon almost all occasions, yet in the greater part of men, taking the whole course of their life at an average, the principle of frugality seems not only to predominate, but to predominate very greatly.

With regard to misconduct, the number of prudent and successful undertakings is everywhere much greater than that of injudicious and unsuccessful ones. After all our complaints of the frequency of bankruptcies, the unhappy men who fall into this misfortune make but a very small part of the whole number engaged in trade, and all other sorts of business; not much more perhaps than one in a thousand. Bankruptcy is perhaps the greatest and most humiliating calamity which can befall an innocent man. The greater part of men, therefore, are sufficiently careful to avoid it. Some, indeed, do not avoid it; as some do not avoid the gallows.

Great nations are never impoverished by private, though they sometimes are by public prodigality and misconduct. The whole, or almost the whole public revenue, is in most countries employed in maintaining unproductive hands. Such are the people who compose a numerous and splendid court, a great ecclesiastical establishment, great fleets and armies, who in time of peace produce nothing, and in time of war acquire nothing which can compensate the expense of maintaining them, even while the war lasts. Such people, as they themselves produce nothing, are all maintained by the produce of other men's labour. When multiplied, therefore, to an unnecessary number, they may in a particular year consume so great a share of this produce, as not to leave a sufficiency for maintaining the productive labourers, who should reproduce it next year. The next year's produce, therefore, will be less than that of the foregoing, and if the same disorder should continue, that of the third year will be still less than that of the second. Those unproductive hands, who should be maintained by a part only of the spare revenue of the people, may consume so great a share of their whole revenue, and thereby oblige so great a number to encroach upon their capitals, upon the funds destined for the maintenance of productive labour, that all the frugality and good conduct of individuals may not be able to compensate the waste and degradation of produce occasioned by this violent and forced encroachment.

This frugality and good conduct, however, is upon most occasions, it appears from experience, sufficient to compensate, not only the private prodigality and misconduct of individuals, but the public extravagance of government. The uniform, constant, and uninterrupted effort of every man to better his condition, the principle from which public and national, as well as private opulence is originally derived, is frequently powerful enough to maintain the natural progress of things towards improvement, in spite both of the extravagance of government and of the greatest errors of administration. Like the unknown principle of animal life, it frequently restores health and vigour to the constitution, in spite, not only of the disease, but of the absurd prescriptions of the doctor.

The annual produce of the land and labour of any nation can be increased in its value by no other means but by increasing either the number of its productive labourers, or the productive powers of those labourers who had before been employed. The number of its productive labourers, it is evident, can never be much increased, but in consequence of an increase of capital, or of the funds destined for maintaining them. The productive powers of the same number of labourers cannot be increased, but in consequence either of some addition and improvement to those machines and instruments which facilitate and abridge labour; or of a more proper division and distribution of employment. In either case an additional capital is almost always required. It is by means of an additional capital only that the undertaker of any work can either provide his workmen with better machinery or make a more proper distribution of employment among them. When the work to be done consists of a number of parts, to keep every man constantly employed in one way requires a much greater capital than where every man is occasionally employed in every different part of the work. When we compare, therefore, the state of a nation at two different periods, and find, that the annual produce of its land and labour is evidently greater at the latter than at the former, that its lands are better cultivated, its manufactures more numerous and more flourishing, and its trade more extensive, we may be assured that its capital must have increased during the interval between those two periods, and that more must have been added to it by the good conduct of some than had been taken from it either by the private misconduct of others or by the public extravagance of government. But we shall find this to have been the case of almost all nations, in all tolerably quiet and peaceable times, even of those who have not enjoyed the most prudent and parsimonious governments. To form a right judgment of it, indeed, we must compare the state of the country at periods somewhat distant from one another. The progress is frequently so gradual that, at near periods, the improvement is not only not sensible, but from the declension either of certain branches of industry, or of certain districts of the country, things which sometimes happen though the country in general be in great prosperity, there frequently arises a suspicion that the riches and industry of the whole are decaying.

The annual produce of the land and labour of England, for example, is certainly much greater than it was, a little more than a century ago, at the restoration of Charles II. Though, at present, few people, I believe, doubt of this, yet during this period, five years have seldom passed away in which some book or pamphlet has not been published, written, too, with such abilities as to gain some authority with the public, and pretending to demonstrate that the wealth of the nation was fast declining, that the country was depopulated, agriculture neglected, manufactures decaying, and trade undone. Nor have these publications been all party pamphlets, the wretched offspring of falsehood and venality. Many of them have been written by very candid and very intelligent people, who wrote nothing but what they believed, and for no other reason but because they believed it.

The annual produce of the land and labour of England, again, was certainly much greater at the Restoration, than we can suppose it to have been about an hundred years before, at the accession of Elizabeth. At this period, too, we have all reason to believe, the country was much more advanced in improvement than it had been about a century before, towards the close of the dissensions between the houses of York and Lancaster. Even then it was, probably, in a better condition than it had been at the Norman Conquest, and at the Norman Conquest than during the confusion of the Saxon Heptarchy. Even at this early period, it was certainly a more improved country than at the invasion of Julius Caesar, when its inhabitants were nearly in the same state with the savages in North America.

In each of those periods, however, there was not only much private and public profusion, many expensive and unnecessary wars, great perversion of the annual produce from maintaining productive to maintain unproductive hands; but sometimes, in the confusion of civil discord, such absolute waste and destruction of stock, as might be supposed, not only to retard, as it certainly did, the natural accumulation of riches, but to have left the country, at the end of the period, poorer than at the beginning. Thus, in the happiest and most fortunate period of them all, that which has passed since the Restoration, how many disorders and misfortunes have occurred, which, could they have been foreseen, not only the impoverishment, but the total ruin of the country would have been expected from them? The fire and the plague of London, the two Dutch wars, the disorders of the Revolution, the war in Ireland, the four expensive French wars of 1688, 1702, 1742, and 1756, together with the two rebellions of 1715 and 1745. In the course of the four French wars, the nation has contracted more than a hundred and forty-five millions of debt, over and above all the other extraordinary annual expense which they occasioned, so that the whole cannot be computed at less than two hundred millions. So great a share of the annual produce of the land and labour of the country has, since the Revolution, been employed upon different occasions in maintaining an extraordinary number of unproductive hands. But had not those wars given this particular direction to so large a capital, the greater part of it would naturally have been employed in maintaining productive hands, whose labour would have replaced, with a profit, the whole value of their consumption. The value of the annual produce of the land and labour of the country would have been considerably increased by it every year, and every year's increase would have augmented still more that of the following year. More houses would have been built, more lands would have been improved, and those which had been improved before would have been better cultivated, more manufactures would have been established. and those which had been established before would have been more extended; and to what height the real wealth and revenue of the country might, by this time, have been raised, it is not perhaps very easy even to imagine.

But though the profusion of government must, undoubtedly, have retarded the natural progress of England towards wealth and improvement, it has not been able to stop it. The annual produce of its land and labour is, undoubtedly, much greater at present than it was either at the Restoration or at the Revolution. The capital, therefore, annually employed in cultivating this land, and in maintaining this labour, must likewise be much greater. In the midst of all the exactions of government, this capital has been silently and gradually accumulated by the private frugality and good conduct of individuals, by their universal, continual, and uninterrupted effort to better their own condition. It is this effort, protected by law and allowed by liberty to exert itself in the manner that is most advantageous, which has maintained the progress of England towards opulence and improvement in almost all former times, and which, it is to be hoped, will do so in all future times. England, however, as it has never been blessed with a very parsimonious government, so parsimony has at no time been the characteristical virtue of its inhabitants. It is the highest impertinence and presumption, therefore, in kings and ministers, to pretend to watch over the economy of private people, and to restrain their expense, either by sumptuary laws, or by prohibiting the importation of foreign luxuries. They are themselves always, and without any exception, the greatest spendthrifts in the society. Let them look well after their own expense, and they may safely trust private people with theirs. If their own extravagance does not ruin the state, that of their subjects never will.

As frugality increases and prodigality diminishes the public capital, so the conduct of those whose expense just equals their revenue, without either accumulating or encroaching, neither increases nor diminishes it. Some modes of expense, however, seem to contribute more to the growth of public opulence than others.

The revenue of an individual may be spent either in things which are consumed immediately, and in which one day's expense can neither alleviate nor support that of another, or it may be spent in things more durable, which can therefore be accumulated, and in which every day's expense may, as he chooses, either alleviate or support and heighten the effect of that of the following day. A man of fortune, for example, may either spend his revenue in a profuse and sumptuous table, and in maintaining a great number of menial servants, and a multitude of dogs and horses; or contenting himself with a frugal table and few attendants, he may lay out the greater part of it in adorning his house or his country villa, in useful or ornamental buildings, in useful or ornamental furniture, in collecting books, statues, pictures; or in things more frivolous, jewels, baubles, ingenious trinkets of different kinds; or, what is most trifling of all, in amassing a great wardrobe of fine clothes, like the favourite and minister of a great prince who died a few years ago. Were two men of equal fortune to spend their revenue, the one chiefly in the one way, the other in the other, the magnificence of the person whose expense had been chiefly in durable commodities, would be continually increasing, every day's expense contributing something to support and heighten the effect of that of the following day: that of the other, on the contrary, would be no greater at the end of the period than at the beginning. The former, too, would, at the end of the period, be the richer man of the two. He would have a stock of goods of some kind or other, which, though it might not be worth all that it cost, would always be worth something. No trace or vestige of the expense of the latter would remain, and the effects of ten or twenty years profusion would be as completely annihilated as if they had never existed.

As the one mode of expense is more favourable than the other to the opulence of an individual, so is it likewise to that of a nation. The houses, the furniture, the clothing of the rich, in a little time, become useful to the inferior and middling ranks of people. They are able to purchase them when their superiors grow weary of them, and the general accommodation of the whole people is thus gradually improved, when this mode of expense becomes universal among men of fortune. In countries which have long been rich, you will frequently find the inferior ranks of people in possession both of houses and furniture perfectly good and entire, but of which neither the one could have been built, nor the other have been made for their use. What was formerly a seat of the family of Seymour is now an inn upon the Bath road. The marriage-bed of James the First of Great Britain, which his queen brought with her from Denmark as a present fit for a sovereign to make to a sovereign, was, a few years ago, the ornament of an alehouse at Dunfermline. In some ancient cities, which either have been long stationary, or have gone somewhat to decay, you will sometimes scarce find a single house which could have been built for its present inhabitants. If you go into those houses too, you will frequently find many excellent, though antiquated pieces of furniture, which are still very fit for use, and which could as little have been made for them. Noble palaces, magnificent villas, great collections of books, statues, pictures and other curiosities, are frequently both an ornament and an honour, not only to the neighbourhood, but to the whole country to which they belong. Versailles is an ornament and an honour to France, Stowe and Wilton to England. Italy still continues to command some sort of veneration by the number of monuments of this kind which it possesses, though the wealth which produced them has decayed, and though the genius which planned them seems to be extinguished, perhaps from not having the same employment.

The expense too, which is laid out in durable commodities, is favourable, not only to accumulation, but to frugality. If a person should at any time exceed in it, he can easily reform without exposing himself to the censure of the public. To reduce very much the number of his servants, to reform his table from great profusion to great frugality, to lay down his equipage after he has once set it up, are changes which cannot escape the observation of his neighbours, and which are supposed to imply some acknowledgment of preceding bad conduct. Few, therefore, of those who have once been so unfortunate as to launch out too far into this sort of expense, have afterwards the courage to reform, till ruin and bankruptcy oblige them. But if a person has, at any time, been at too great an expense in building, in furniture, in books or pictures, no imprudence can be inferred from his changing his conduct. These are things in which further expense is frequently rendered unnecessary by former expense; and when a person stops short, he appears to do so, not because he has exceeded his fortune, but because he has satisfied his fancy.

The expense, besides, that is laid out in durable commodities gives maintenance, commonly, to a greater number of people than that which is employed in the most profuse hospitality. Of two or three hundredweight of provisions, which may sometimes be served up at a great festival, one half, perhaps, is thrown to the dunghill, and there is always a great deal wasted and abused. But if the expense of this entertainment had been employed in setting to work masons, carpenters, upholsterers, mechanics, etc., a quantity of provisions, of equal value, would have been distributed among a still greater number of people who would have bought them in pennyworths and pound weights, and not have lost or thrown away a single ounce of them. In the one way, besides, this expense maintains productive, in the other unproductive hands. In the one way, therefore, it increases, in the other, it does not increase, the exchangeable value of the annual produce of the land and labour of the country.

I would not, however, by all this be understood to mean that the one species of expense always betokens a more liberal or generous spirit than the other. When a man of fortune spends his revenue chiefly in hospitality, he shares the greater part of it with his friends and companions; but when he employs it in purchasing such durable commodities, he often spends the whole upon his own person, and gives nothing to anybody without an equivalent. The latter species of expense, therefore, especially when directed towards frivolous objects, the little ornaments of dress and furniture, jewels, trinkets, gewgaws, frequently indicates, not only a trifling, but a base and selfish

disposition. All that I mean is, that the one sort of expense, as it always occasions some accumulation of valuable commodities, as it is more favourable to private frugality, and, consequently, to the increase of the public capital, and as it maintains productive, rather than unproductive hands, conduces more than the other to the growth of public opulence.
'The Wealth of Nations,' Book 2, Chapter 3.

PRINCIPAL WORKS OF ADAM SMITH

Theory of Moral Sentiments 1759
An Inquiry into the Nature and Causes of the Wealth of Nations 1776
Essays on Philosophical Subjects 1795